Level 2 • Book 2

Fossils

•

Courage

•

Our Country and Its People

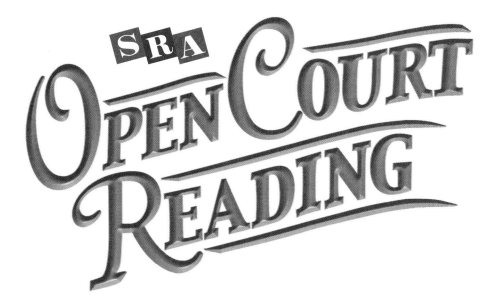

SRA OPEN COURT READING

Level 2 • Book 2

— **PROGRAM AUTHORS** —

Carl Bereiter	Michael Pressley	Joe Campione
Marilyn Jager Adams	Marsha Roit	Iva Carruthers
Marlene Scardamalia	Jan Hirshberg	Gerald H. Treadway, Jr.
	Anne McKeough	

A Division of The **McGraw-Hill** Companies

Columbus, Ohio

Acknowledgments

Grateful acknowledgement is given to the following publishers and copyright owners for permissions granted to reprint selections from their publications. All possible care has been taken to trace ownership and secure permission for each selection included. In case of any errors or omissions, the Publisher will be pleased to make suitable acknowledgements in future editions.

FOSSILS

FOSSILS TELL OF LONG AGO by Aliki Brandenberg. COPYRIGHT ©1972, 1990 BY ALIKI BRANDENBERG. Used by permission of HarperCollins Publishers.

From THE DINOSAUR WHO LIVED IN MY BACKYARD by B.G. Hennessy, copyright © 1988 by B.G. Hennessy, text. Used by permission of Viking Penguin, an imprint of Penguin Putnam Books for Young Readers, a division of Penguin Putnam Inc. From THE DINOSAUR WHO LIVED IN MY BACKYARD by B.G. Hennessy, pictures by Susan Davis, copyright © 1988 by Susan Davis, illustrations. Used by permission of Viking Penguin, an imprint of Penguin Putnam Books for Young Readers, a division of Penguin Putnam Inc.

"Iguanadon" from TYRANNOSAURUS WAS A BEAST by Jack Prelutsky. TEXT COPYRIGHT ©1988 BY JACK PRELUTSKY. Used by permission of HarperCollins Publishers.

"Seismosaurus" from TYRANNOSAURUS WAS A BEAST by Jack Prelutsky. TEXT COPYRIGHT ©1988 BY JACK PRELUTSKY. Used by permission of HarperCollins Publishers.

From Dinosaur Fossils, by Alvin Granowsky. Copyright © 1992 by Steck-Vaughn Company. Reproduced by arrangement with Steck-Vaughn Company.

"Fossils" from SOMETHING NEW BEGINS by Lilian Moore. Copyright © 1982 Lilian Moore. Used by permission of Marian Reiner for the author. Illustration from DINOSAURS by Lee Bennett Hopkins, illustrations copyright © 1987 by Murray Tinkelman, reproduced by permission of Harcourt, Inc.

"Monster Tracks" from Cricket the Magazine for Children, text & art copyright 1991 by Barbara Bruno. Reprinted with permission of copyright holder.

From LET'S GO DINOSAUR TRACKING, copyright © 1991 by Miriam Schlein. Reprinted by permission of S©ott Treimel NY. Illustrations copyright © 1991 by Kate Duke. Used by permission of the artist.

COURAGE

MOLLY THE BRAVE AND ME Text copyright © 1990 by Jane O'Connor. Illustrations copyright ©1990 by Sheila Hamanaka. Published by arrangement with Random House Children's books, a division of Random House, Inc., New York, New York. All rights reserved.

From HOCKEY CARDS & HOPSCOTCH & STUDY BOOK, by Emily Hearn © 1971. Reprinted with permission of Nelson Thompson Learning a division of Thompson Learning. Fax 800 730-2215.

"Dragons and Giants" from FROG AND TOAD TOGETHER COPYRIGHT © 1971, 1972 BY ARNOLD LOBEL. Used by permission of HarperCollins Publishers.

"Life Doesn't Frighten Me" from AND STILL I RISE by Maya Angelou. Copyright ©1978 by Maya Angelou. Reprinted by permission of Random House, Inc.

From THE HOLE IN THE DIKE by Norma Green, illustrated by Eric Carle. Text copyright © 1974 by Norma Green, illustrations copyright © 1974 by Eric Carle. Reprinted by permission of Scholastic Inc.

A PICTURE BOOK OF MARTIN LUTHER KING, JR. Text copyright ©1989 by David A. Adler. Illustrations copyright ©1989 by Robert Casilla. All rights reserved. Reprinted by permission of Holiday House, Inc.

From THE EMPTY POT by Demi. Copyright, © 1990 by Demi. Reprinted by permission of Henry Holt and Company, LLC.

BRAVE AS A MOUNTAIN LION by Ann Herbert Scott. Text copyright ©1996 by Ann Herbert Scott. Illustrations copyright © 1996 by Glo Coalson. Reprinted by permission of Clarion Books/Houghton Mifflin Co. All rights reserved.

OUR COUNTRY AND ITS PEOPLE

From THE FIRST AMERICANS, text copyright © 1980 by Jane Werner Watson, illustrations copyright © 1980 by Troy Howell. Published by arrangement with Random House Children's Books a division of Random House, Inc., New York, New York. All rights reserved.

NEW HOPE by Henri Sorensen. COPYRIGHT © 1995 BY HENRI SORENSEN. Used by permission of HarperCollins Publishers.

From A PLACE CALLED FREEDOM. Text copyright © 1997 by Scott Russell Sanders; illustrations copyright © 1997 by Thomas B. Allen. Reprinted with permission of Atheneum Books for Young Readers, Simon & Schuster Chldren's Publishing Division. All right

THE STORY OF THE STATUE OF LIBERTY by Betsy Maestro. Illustrated by Giulio Maestro. Text copyright © 1986 by Betsy Maestro. Illustrations copyright © 1986 by Giulio Maestro. Used by permission of HarperCollins Publishers.

"Statue of Liberty" reprinted with the permission of Margaret K. McElderry Books, an imprint of Simon & Schuster Children's Publishing Division from I NEVER TOLD AND OTHER POEMS by Myra Cohn Livingston. Copyright ©1992 Myra Cohn Livingston.

THE BUTTERFLY SEEDS COPYRIGHT © 1995 BY MARY WATSON. Used by permission of HarperCollins Publishers.

From A PIECE OF HOME by Sonia Levitin, copyright © 1996, Illustrations copyright © 1996 by Juan Wijngaard. Used by permission of Dial Books for Young Readers, an imprint of Penguin Putnam Books for Young Readers, a division of Penguin Putnam Inc.

From JALAPEÑO BAGELS. Text copyright © 1996 by Natasha Wing, illustrations copyright ©1996 by Robert Casilla. Reprinted with permission of Atheneum Books for Young Readers, Simon & Schuster Children's Publishing Division. All rights reserved.

www.sra4kids.com

SRA/McGraw-Hill

A Division of The McGraw-Hill Companies

Send all inquiries to:
SRA/McGraw-Hill
8787 Orion Place
Columbus, Ohio 43240-4027

Printed in the United States of America.

ISBN 0-07-569245-7

8 9 RRW 04

— PROGRAM AUTHORS —

Carl Bereiter, Ph.D.
University of Toronto

Marilyn Jager Adams, Ph.D.
BBN Technologies

Michael Pressley, Ph.D.
University of Notre Dame

Marsha Roit, Ph.D.
National Reading Consultant

Anne McKeough, Ph.D.
University of Toronto

Jan Hirshberg, Ed.D.
Reading Specialist

Marlene Scardamalia, Ph.D.
University of Calgary

Joe Campione, Ph.D.
University of California at Berkeley

Iva Carruthers, Ph.D.
Northeastern Illinois University

Gerald H. Treadway, Jr., Ed.D.
San Diego State University

UNIT 4

Table of Contents

T--ble of Cont--nts

Table of Contents
Our Country and Its People 246

How do you know things like dinosaurs lived many, many years ago? How can we tell how big they were or what they looked like? Fossils can be the keys to the past. Find out what scientists see in fossils of long ago.

FOSSILS
Tell of Long Ago

by Aliki

Once upon a time a huge fish was swimming
around when along came a smaller fish. The
big fish was so hungry it swallowed the
other fish whole. The big fish died and sank
to the bottom of the sea.

This happened ninety million years ago. How
do we know?

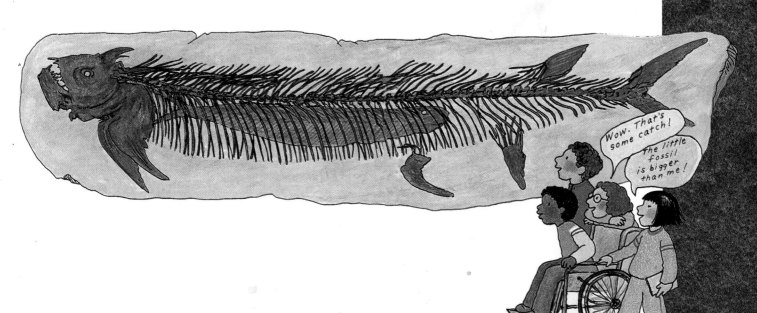

We know because the fish turned to stone. The fish became a fossil. A plant or animal that has turned to stone is called a fossil.

Scientists can tell how old stones are. They could tell how old the fish fossil was.

How did the fish become a fossil? Most animals and plants do not become fossils when they die. Some rot. Others dry up, crumble, and blow away. No trace of them is left. This could have happened to the big fish. We would never know it had lived.

Instead, the fish became a fossil. This is how it happened.

When the big fish died, it sank into the mud at the bottom of the sea. Slowly, the soft parts of the fish rotted away. Only its hard bones were left. The bones of the fish it had eaten were left, too. The skeleton of the fish lay buried and protected deep in the mud.

Thousands of years went by. More layers of mud covered the fish. Tons and tons of mud piled up. After a long time, the surface of the earth changed. The sea where the fish was buried dried out. The weight of the layers of mud pressed down. Slowly, the mud turned to rock.

As that happened, ground water seeped through the changing layers of mud. Minerals were dissolved in the water. The water seeped into all the tiny holes in the fish bones. The minerals in the water were left behind in the fish bones.

After a very long time the bones turned to stone. The fish was a fossil.

Some fossils, like the fish, are actual parts of plants or animals that have turned to stone. Sometimes a fossil is only an imprint of a plant or animal.

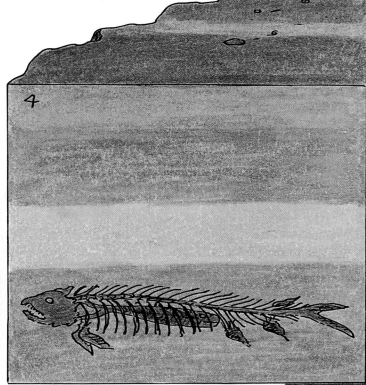

Millions of years ago, a leaf fell off a fernlike plant. It dropped onto the swampy forest soil, which is called peat. The leaf rotted away. But if left the mark of its shape in the peat. The peat, with the imprint of the leaf, hardened. It became a rock called coal. Coal is a fossil, too.

These are dinosaur tracks. They were made in fresh mud 115 million years ago.

Sand filled the dinosaur's footprints in the mud.

The sand hardened into a rock called sandstone. Millions of years later fossil hunters dug through the rock. They found the fossil tracks—exact imprints of the dinosaur's foot.

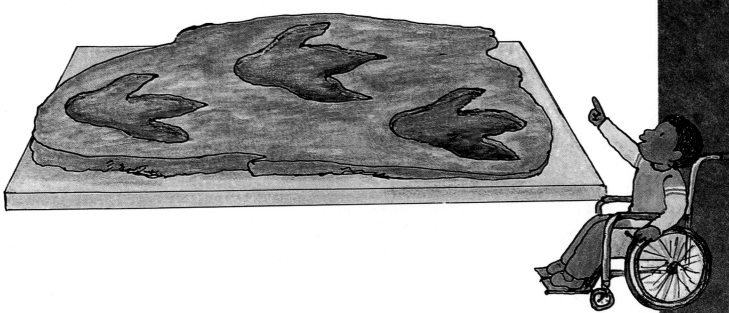

Not all fossils are found in stone. Some are found in the frozen ground of the Arctic. This ancient mammoth was a kind of elephant. It froze to death thousands of years ago. The grass it had been eating was still in its mouth!

Millions of years ago, a fly was caught in the sticky sap of a tree. The sap hardened and became a fossil called amber. Amber looks like yellow glass. The fly was perfectly preserved in the amber. Other insects have been preserved in amber, too.

We have learned many things from the fish, the fern, the fly, and the dinosaur tracks. Fossils tell us about the past.

Fossils tell us there once were forests where now there are deserts. Fossils tell us there once were seas where now there are mountains.

Many lands that are cold today were once warm. We find fossils of tropical plants in very cold places.

Fossils tell us about strange creatures that lived on earth long ago. No such creatures are alive today. They have all died out. We say they are extinct.

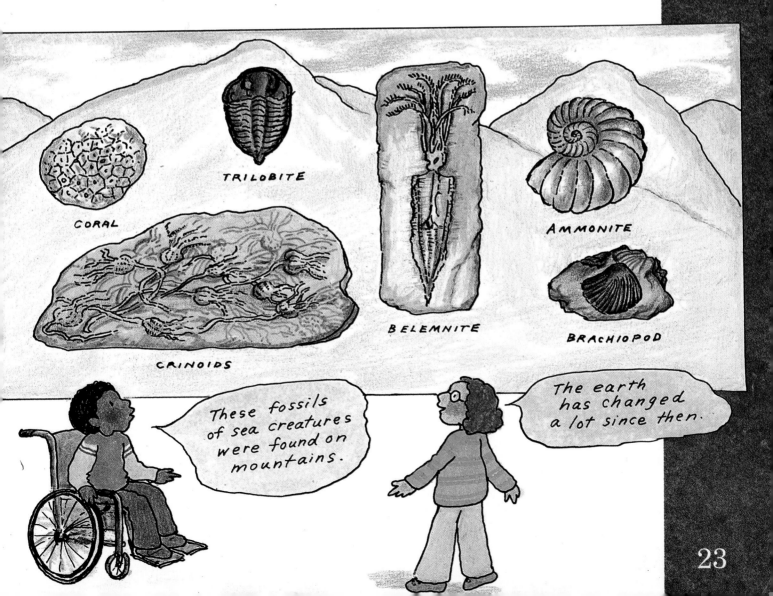

CORAL

TRILOBITE

BELEMNITE

AMMONITE

BRACHIOPOD

CRINOIDS

These fossils of sea creatures were found on mountains.

The earth has changed a lot since then.

Some fossils are found by scientists who dig for them. Some fossils are found by accident.

You, too, might find a fossil if you look hard. When you see a stone, look at it carefully. It may be a fossil of something that once lived.

How would you like to make a fossil? Not a one-million-year-old fossil. A one-minute-old fossil.

Make a clay imprint of your hand. The imprint shows what your hand is like, the way a dinosaur's track shows us what its foot was like.

First you take some clay.

Then you flatten it out.

Press your hand in the clay.

Then lift your hand away.

Suppose, when it dried out, you buried your clay imprint. Suppose a million years from now, someone found it. Your imprint would be as hard as stone. It would be a fossil of your hand. It would tell the finder something about you. It would tell something about life on earth, a million years earlier.

I hereby bury you, fossil.

Every time someone finds a fossil, we learn more about life on earth long ago. Someday you may find a fossil—one that is millions and millions of years old. You may discover something no one knows today.

27

FOSSILS
Tell of Long Ago

Meet the Author and Illustrator

Aliki Brandenberg loves to write and draw. When she is curious about something, she writes a non-fiction book. She writes fiction books from experiences she has had. Aliki Brandenberg feels very lucky to spend her life doing what she loves!

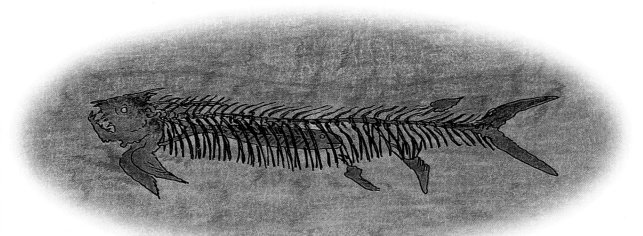

Theme Connections

Within the Selection

Writer's Notebook Record your answers to the questions below in the Response Journal section of your Writer's Notebook. In small groups, report the ideas you wrote. Discuss your ideas with the rest of the group. Then choose a person to report your group's answers to the class.

- What are fossils?
- Why are fossils important discoveries?

Beyond the Selection

- Have you ever seen fossils in a museum? What kinds of fossils did you see?
- Think about what "Fossils Tell of Long Ago" tells you about fossils.
- Add items to the Concept/Question Board about fossils.

Focus Questions What is the difference between fact and opinion? Is it possible that a dinosaur once lived in your backyard?

The Dinosaur Who Lived in My Backyard

B. G. Hennessy
illustrated by Susan Davis

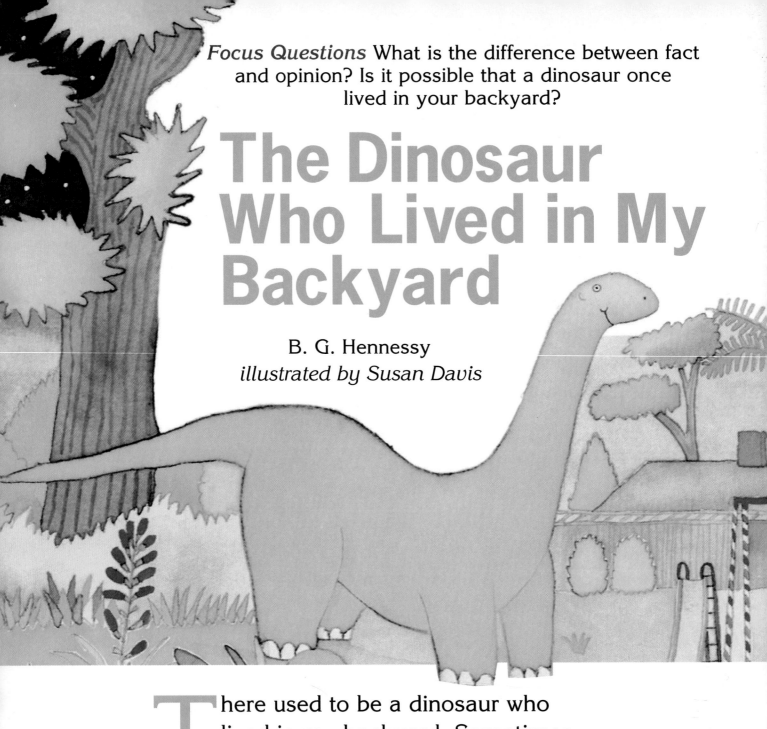

There used to be a dinosaur who lived in my backyard. Sometimes I wish he still lived here.
The dinosaur who lived here hatched from an egg that was as big as a basketball.

By the time he was five, he was as big
as our car.

Just one of his dinosaur feet was so big
it wouldn't even have fit in my sandbox.

My mother says that if you eat all your vegetables you'll grow very strong. That must be true, because that's all this dinosaur ate. I bet he ate a hundred pounds of vegetables every day. That's a whole lot of lima beans.

This dinosaur was so heavy that he would have made my whole neighborhood shake like pudding if he jumped. He weighed as much as twenty pick-up trucks.

The dinosaur who lived in my backyard was bigger than my schoolbus. Even bigger than my house.

He had many other dinosaur friends. Sometimes they played hide-and-seek. Sometimes they had terrible fights.

The dinosaur who used to live here was allowed to sleep outside every night. It's a good thing he didn't need a tent. He was so big he would have needed a circus tent to keep him covered.

Back when my dinosaur lived here,
my town was a big swamp. This dinosaur
needed a lot of water. If he still lived
here we'd have to keep the sprinkler on
all the time.

My dinosaur had a very long neck so he could eat the leaves at the top of trees. If he still lived here, I bet he could rescue my kite.

That's all I know about the dinosaur who used to live in my backyard.

He hasn't been around for a very long time. Sometimes I wish he still lived here.

It would be pretty hard to keep a dinosaur happy.

But my sister and I are saving all our lima beans—just in case.

The Dinosaur Who Lived in My Backyard

Meet the Author

B. G. Hennessy worked as a book designer and an art director for children's books. She began writing books when her first child was learning to talk. As she writes, she thinks about how the picture would look. She tries to give the illustrator something to work with. She wrote her first book when she was five years old. She still has this book and often reads it to children in schools.

Meet the Illustrator

Susan Davis always wanted to do children's books. Unlike many other artists who studied art in school, she studied art on her own. She said, *"The important thing in illustrating a book is to be patient."* "The Dinosaur Who Lived in My Backyard" took two years to illustrate. She wanted to show the dinosaur doing all sorts of things. She has also illustrated other children's books.

Theme Connections

Within the Selection

Writer's Notebook Record your answers to the questions below in the Response Journal section of your Writer's Notebook. In small groups, report the ideas you wrote. Discuss your ideas with the rest of the group. Then choose a person to report your group's answers to the class.

- Is it possible that a dinosaur really lived in the boy's backyard? How could you know for sure?
- Would a city in our world today make a good home for a dinosaur? Why or why not?

Across Selections

- Think about what you learned in "Fossils Tell of Long Ago." If a dinosaur did live in the boy's backyard, what kind of evidence might it have left?

Beyond the Selection

- What kinds of creatures do you think lived in your neighborhood long ago? How could you find out?
- Think about how "The Dinosaur Who Lived in My Backyard" adds to what you know about fossils.
- Add items to the Concept/Question Board about fossils.

Iguanodon

Jack Prelutsky
illustrated by Daniel Moreton

Iguanodon, Iguanodon,
whatever made you fade,
you've traveled on, Iguanodon,
we wish you could have stayed.

Iguanodon, Iguanodon,
we've sought you everywhere,
both here and yon, Iguanodon,
but failed to find you there.

Iguanodon, Iguanodon,
you were a gentle kind,
but now you're gone, Iguanodon,
and left your bones behind.

40

Seismosaurus

Jack Prelutsky
illustrated by Daniel Moreton

Seismosaurus was enormous,
Seismosaurus was tremendous,
Seismosaurus was prodigious,
Seismosaurus was stupendous.

Seismosaurus was titanic,
Seismosaurus was colossal,
Seismosaurus now is nothing
but a monumental fossil.

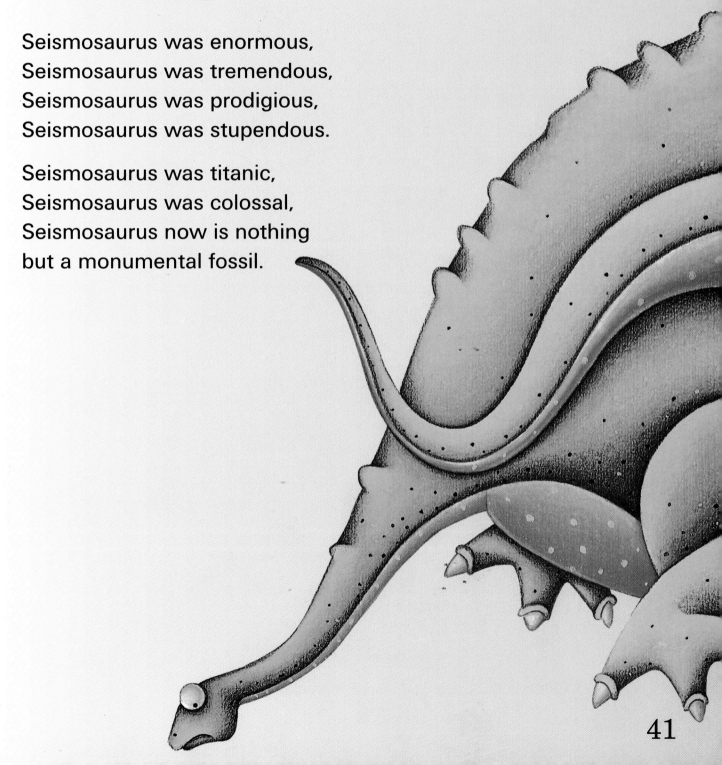

41

Dinosaur Fossils

by Dr. Alvin Granowsky

We have learned all that we know about dinosaurs from their fossils. A fossil is what is left of a plant or an animal that lived long ago.

Fossils can be leaves, shells, eggs, or skeletons. Some fossils are hardened tracks or footprints left by a moving animal.

When a plant or animal dies, it can become covered with mud or sand. As time goes by, the plant or animal becomes covered by many layers of mud and sand. After thousands of years, the bottom layers harden into rock. The dead plant or animal also hardens into rock. This is how fossils are formed.

Any plant or animal can become a fossil. Animal fossils are usually hard parts of the body such as teeth, bones, or shells.

Sometimes an animal's whole body is frozen in ice or covered very quickly with river mud. Then scientists can study the skin and other soft parts of an animal's body.

Sometimes fossils are found by chance.
Fossils may be uncovered by workers digging
a well or roadway.

Most often, scientists who study fossils
have to spend a long time looking for them.
These scientists are called paleontologists.

Fossils found in soft ground are the easiest ones to collect. Paleontologists can dig them out with a shovel or by hand.

Fossils have to be loosened slowly from rocks. Scientists use chisels, hammers, or picks to remove the fossils. They work carefully to protect the fossils.

Then the hardest work begins. Most fossils are found in pieces. The bones are like the pieces of a puzzle. Putting the bones together is difficult when some of the pieces are missing.

What if some of the fossil pieces don't belong? That often happens when the fossils of many animals are found in the same place.

Sometimes scientists make mistakes when they work with fossils. At one time, they thought the thumb-claw of an Iguanodon was a horn on its nose.

But scientists learn from their mistakes. They work until they find the right way to put the bones together. The skeletons are placed in museums so that everyone can learn about dinosaurs.

Scientists must learn about dinosaurs from fossils because dinosaurs are extinct. When scientists say that dinosaurs are extinct they mean that dinosaurs are not alive today.

For a long time, we didn't know that dinosaurs had ever lived. Then dinosaur fossils were found. Scientists learned that dinosaurs had once lived all over Earth.

When the first dinosaur fossils were found, people wondered, "What kind of bone is this?"

People saw how big the bones were. They asked, "Could these be the bones of an elephant?"

Putting together dinosaur bones was slow work. Scientists tried putting the bones together in different ways.

If some of a dinosaur's bones were missing, the job was even slower. Sometimes scientists had to guess what the missing parts looked like.

At one time, scientists thought they had discovered a new dinosaur called a Polacanthus. Scientists had only part of the skeleton, but they tried to imagine what a Polacanthus looked like. They thought that the Polacanthus had a small head and spikes along its back.

But later, scientists found other bones that belonged to the same skeleton. With the new bones, scientists could see that the skeleton was from a Hylaeosaurus.

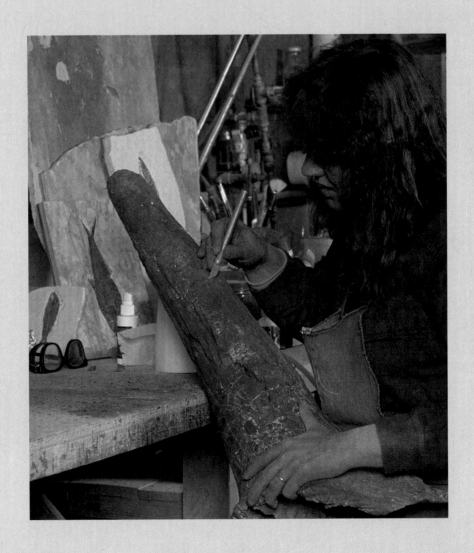

Sometimes scientists find many dinosaur bones in one place. In Wyoming, scientists discovered several complete skeletons of Camptosaurus dinosaurs. That made it easier to describe a Camptosaurus. After studying the skeletons, scientists decided that the Camptosaurus grew as long as 23 feet.

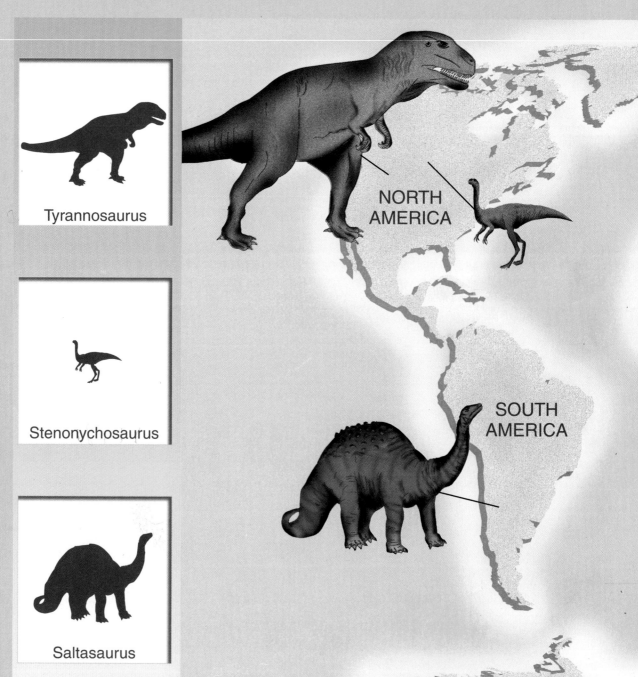

Tyrannosaurus

Stenonychosaurus

Saltasaurus

NORTH AMERICA

SOUTH AMERICA

Dinosaur fossils have been found in many places around the world. That is how we know that dinosaurs once lived all over Earth. This map shows where the fossils of some kinds of dinosaurs were found.

EUROPE

ASIA

AFRICA

AUSTRALIA

ANTARCTICA

Iguanodon

Velociraptor

Vulcanodon

Dinosaur bones show us that there were dinosaurs of all shapes and sizes. The skeletons scientists put together help us see how different each kind of dinosaur was.

The skeleton of a Tyrannosaurus Rex stands on two legs and has big, sharp teeth. The skeleton of an Apatosaurus shows its long, thin neck and tail.

New fossils are still being found today. Someday you could be a scientist and put together a dinosaur skeleton.

Dinosaur Fossils

Meet the Author

Dr. Alvin Granowsky tested his story ideas for "Dinosaur Fossils" on his young grandson, who really liked dinosaurs and fossils. Dr. Granowsky finds the subject of dinosaurs very exciting. Dinosaurs have been around for a very long time, but new things are still being learned about them.

Dr. Granowsky also likes to tell stories from another point of view. For example, in the story of Cinderella he likes to tell the story from the stepsisters' point of view. He said, *"When I am writing . . . I like to sneak in something that would make someone smile or think."*

Theme Connections

Within the Selection

Writer's Notebook

Record your answers to the questions below in the Response Journal section of your Writer's Notebook. In small groups, report the ideas you wrote. Discuss your ideas with the rest of the group. Then choose a person to report your group's answers to the class.

- Since no one has ever seen a live dinosaur, how do we know what dinosaurs look like?
- What can dinosaur fossils teach us?

Across Selections

- What kind of scientist could help the boy in "The Dinosaur Who Lived in My Backyard" find out if a dinosaur really did live in his backyard? What would the scientist do?
- What does "Dinosaur Fossils" tell you about the dinosaur bones in "Fossils Tell of Long Ago"?

Beyond the Selection

- Think about how "Dinosaur Fossils" adds to what you know about fossils.
- Add items to the Concept/Question Board about fossils.

Focus Questions What stories could fossils tell?
Do you like learning about the past?

Fossils

Lilian Moore
illustrated by Murray Tinkelman

Older than
books,
than scrolls,

older
than the first
tales told

or the
first words
spoken

are the stories

in forests that
turned to
stone

in ice walls
that trapped the
mammoth

in the long
bones of
dinosaurs—

the fossil
stories that begin
Once upon a time

Why Did the Dinosaurs Disappear?

Karen Sapp
illustrated by Robert Frank

Once dinosaurs lived on the earth. Then they disappeared or died out. What happened to them?

64

Many other animals, including animals that lived in the sea and animals that flew through the air also died out. Many plants died too.

No one knows for sure what happened, but scientists have some ideas.

Some scientists think that new kinds of plants started growing because of changes in the climate. Their idea is that these plants poisoned dinosaurs that ate them. Then meat-eating dinosaurs starved to death when they could not find plant-eating dinosaurs to eat. There is a problem with this idea. Only land animals would have eaten the poisonous plants, but sea animals died, too. Besides, this idea does not explain why some kinds of plants also died out.

Did other animals cause the death of the dinosaurs? Maybe small animals stole and ate dinosaur eggs before they could hatch. This would explain what happened to dinosaurs that laid eggs. But what about dinosaurs that were born live? What about the sea animals and plants that died, too?

Many scientists think that the dinosaurs died out because the earth became very cold. Most dinosaurs could not live in very cold weather. They did not have fur or feathers to keep them warm. Dinosaurs were so huge they could not burrow into the ground for warmth and protection. But what could make the weather become so cold?

The earth long ago was not at all like it is today. Huge earthquakes made the water in the oceans rise and fall many times. When the water level fell, there was more moisture in the air. This caused more rain and colder weather. The earthquakes also made volcanoes erupt all over the world. Some scientists think that a giant volcano in the part of the world we now call India erupted for many, many years!

All this time, it blew so much ash and dust into the air that the sun's rays could not reach the earth. Imagine what it would be like never to see the sun! The earth grew very cold. Plants died without the sunlight. Without plants to eat, the plant-eating dinosaurs died. Then the meat-eaters died.

In 1978, a new discovery gave some scientists another idea about why the earth became so cold.

Scientists found a thin layer of clay in many places all over the world. The clay is made up of dust from the time the dinosaurs were dying out. This clay has large amounts of a very rare metal, called *iridium*, that is usually deep inside the earth. When iridium is found near the earth's surface, it usually came from space, in the form of meteorites.

Meteorites are chunks of stone or metal that have crashed to the earth. Most of the time, meteorites do not hit the earth hard enough to do much damage. Sometimes, though, a very large meteorite crashes. When this happens, it makes a huge hole, or *crater*, in the ground.

In 1980, a crater was found in Mexico. Scientists think the crater was made about the time the dinosaurs disappeared. They think the meteorite that caused this crater was 6 miles long.

North America

Mexico

Gulf of Mexico

Mérida

Mexico City

Campeche

Pacific Ocean

South America

Imagine something that big hitting the earth! It would blast millions of tons of dust and rock into the sky. Heat caused by the crash would start many fires. The smoke from those fires would add soot to the air. (Scientists found large amounts of soot mixed in with the iridium.)

The thick cloud of dust, rock, and smoke would swirl around the world, blocking the sunlight for months or even years. Without sunlight, the earth would grow very cold. When the dust finally settled, it would form a layer of clay, and in the clay there would be large amounts of iridium. This is exactly what some scientists think happened. Again, their idea is that the lack of sunshine caused dinosaurs and other life forms to die.

Some scientists think that both the volcano idea and the meteorite idea could be correct. There are two ways this might work. One is that a meteorite might have hit the earth hard enough to make the volcanoes erupt. Another way is that the volcanoes could have been erupting for many years, slowly killing plants and animals. Then, when a meteorite hit, it quickly finished the job.

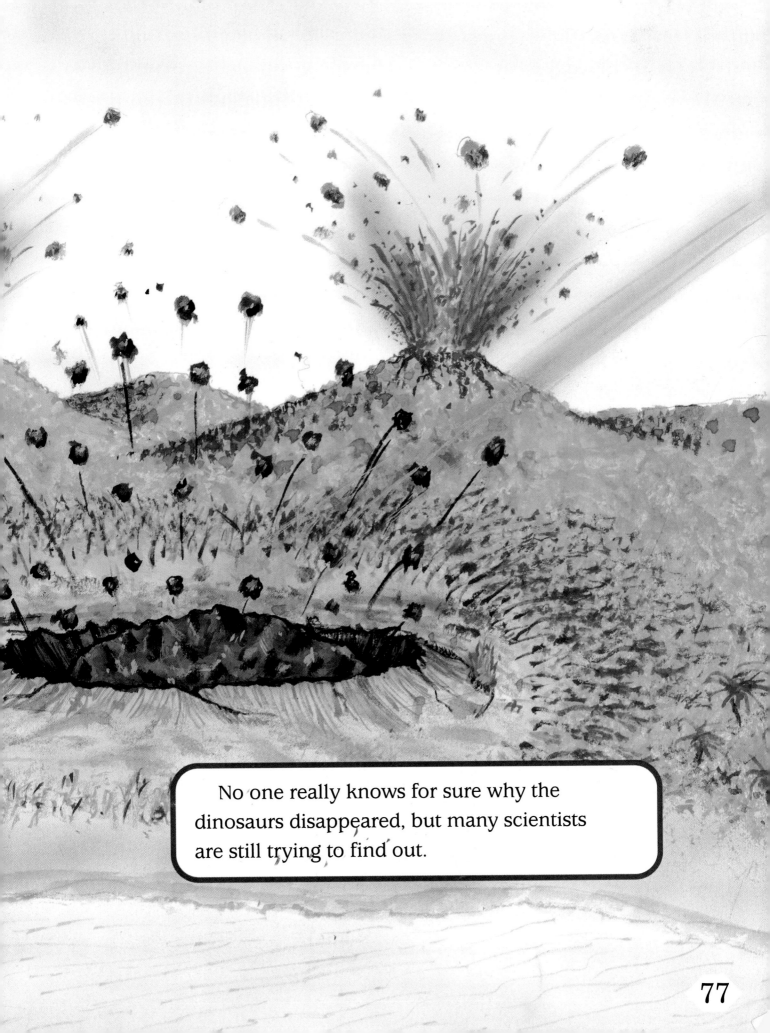

No one really knows for sure why the dinosaurs disappeared, but many scientists are still trying to find out.

Why Did the Dinosaurs Disappear?

Meet the Illustrator

Robert Frank was born in Argentina and moved to the United States during World War II. He grew up in New York City and pursued his interests in art throughout his youth. Attending the High School of Industrial Arts, he went on to study illustration and advertising.

Robert now teaches art at the same school he attended, while he continues to work on freelance illustration projects. He lives in New Jersey with his wife and young daughter and collects antiques as a hobby.

Theme Connections

Within the Selection

Writer's Notebook Record your answers to the questions below in the Response Journal section of your Writer's Notebook. In small groups, report the ideas you wrote. Discuss your ideas with the rest of the group. Then choose a person to report your group's answers to the class.

- How do fossils help scientists form theories about the disappearance of the dinosaurs?
- Scientists have many different theories about why the dinosaurs disappeared. Which theory makes sense to you? Why?

Across Selections

- Based on what you learned in "Fossils Tell of Long Ago" and "Dinosaur Fossils," where can you go to find out more about why the dinosaurs disappeared?
- Do you think the boy in "The Dinosaur Who Lived in My Backyard" would be interested in reading "Why Did the Dinosaurs Disappear?" Why?

Beyond the Selection

- Think about how "Why Did the Dinosaurs Disappear?" adds to what you know about fossils.
- Add items to the Concept/Question Board about fossils.

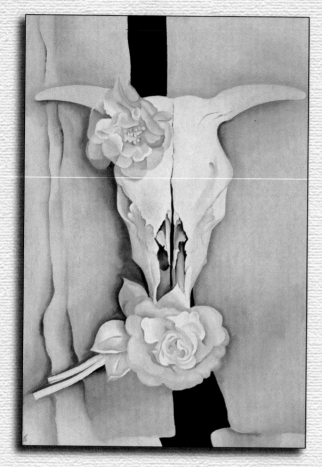

Cow's Skull with Calico Roses. 1932. **Georgia O'Keeffe.** Oil on canvas. 91.2 × 61 cm. The Art Institute of Chicago © 2001 The Georgia O'Keeffe Foundation/Artist's Right Society (ARS), New York.

Desert Still Life. 1951. **Thomas Hart Benton.** Tempera with oil on linen mounted on panel. The Nelson-Atkins Museum of Art, Kansas City, Missouri. ©2001 Thomas Hart Benton and Rita P. Benton Testamentary Trust/Licensed by VAGA, New York, NY.

Fossil of an extinct ancestor of the crayfish, found in the Hummelberg Quarry, Solnhofen, Germany.
Photo: ©Jonathan Blair/Corbis.

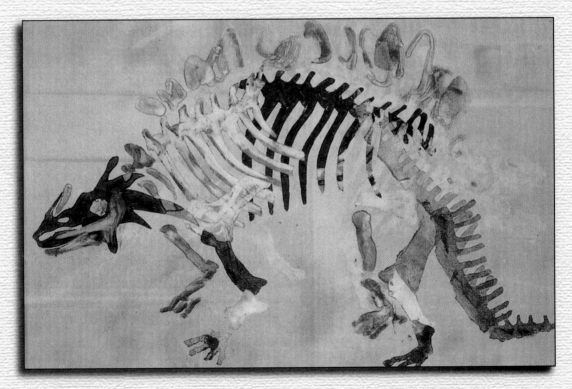

Dinosaur. 1980. **Mary Frank.** Color monotype. 24.75 × 35.5 in. Collection of The Whitney Museum of American Art.

Focus Questions Are fossils still being formed today? Knowing how fossils are made, how would you make a fossil of your own?

Monster Tracks

by Barbara Bruno

Snarl. *Splash. Plop. Eek! Crunch.* Just how did those bones and footprints come to be in these fossil rocks—rocks that tell a wordless story lost in time?

Sand-cast your own fossil clues from a past when monsters roamed and left odd tracks and dinner crumbs in the prehistoric ooze. First gather some feathers, twigs, bones (fish bones are fun), seashells, stones, or small sharp rocks to imprint or embed in sand.

Along with this interesting assortment of objects, you'll also need enough plaster of Paris to fill a mold, sand for shaping the mold, and a container. A plastic-lined, shallow cardboard box works well.

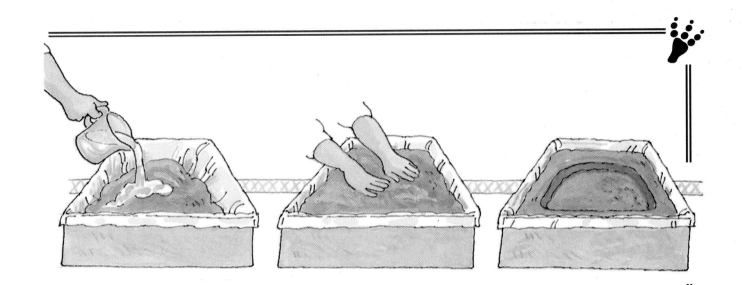

Wet the sand enough so that it keeps its shape when squeezed into a ball, then pack it into the box. Scoop out a flat area about an inch deep and as large as you want your fossil rock to be. Smooth the surface. You're ready to begin sand-casting.

To form the mold you must think in reverse. Holes poked in the sand will stick out. Sunken areas, like footprints, must be built up in the sand. Textures and other features can be made by pressing different objects into the sand. Seashells, bones, and other objects to be left in the sand casting must be pressed facedown into the sand. That way they'll rise above the finished casting's surface. (Half-buried things are interesting, too.)

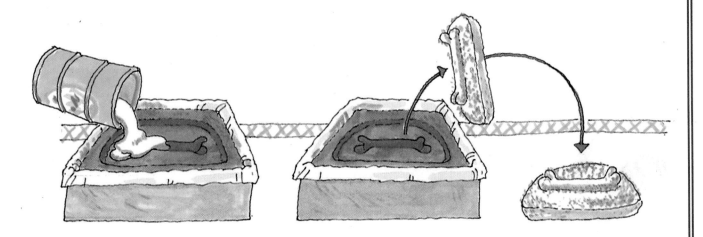

When you have finished making the mold, mix the plaster according to the instructions on the box. Mix only the amount you'll need to fill the mold. Slowly pour the plaster into the deepest parts of the mold first so that trapped air won't spoil the sand casting. Then carefully fill the rest of the mold.

When the sand casting has hardened completely (about fifteen minutes, depending on its size and thickness), carefully dig it up. Gently brush away as much of the sand as you can. Some sand will remain embedded in the plaster.

Your sand casting most likely won't look exactly as you expected, but the results are always fun to see. You can "age" your fossil rock by painting it with watercolors or rubbing mud into the deepest imprints.

Monster Tracks

Meet the Author and Illustrator

Barbara Bruno is a writer, illustrator, and photographer. She studied art at the Philadelphia College of Art. She has illustrated over fifty craft articles for a magazine for children called *Cricket*. She lives in New Jersey.

Theme Connections

Within the Selection

Writer's Notebook Record your answers to the questions below in the Response Journal section of your Writer's Notebook. In small groups, report the ideas you wrote. Discuss your ideas with the rest of the group. Then choose a person to report your group's answers to the class.

- How can you make your own fossil?
- What is the reason for painting or rubbing mud on your imprint when you're making the fossil?

Across Selections

- How are the fossils in "Fossils Tell of Long Ago" and "Dinosaur Fossils" different from a fossil you could make yourself?

Beyond the Selection

- If you were to make your own fossil, what objects would you use?
- Think about how "Monster Tracks" adds to what you know about fossils.
- Add items to the Concept/Question Board about fossils.

Focus Questions What clues can fossils give us?
Have all the important fossils already been discovered?

LET'S GO DINOSAUR TRACKING!

Miriam Schlein

illustrated by Kate Duke

Put on your boots.
Put on your pith helmet.
And take some water in a canteen.
We're going to do some dinosaur tracking.

Here's the first set of tracks.
Who made them,
and what do they tell us?
We know one thing right away.
Each footprint is 38 inches long.
Whoever made these tracks
sure was big.
And heavy!
Look how deep the footprints are.
We can stand in them.
There's a fish swimming in one!
Who made these giant steps?

More than 100 million years ago a big sauropod walked by along a mud flat by the side of a lagoon. The feet that made these footprints carried a 70-foot-long 30-ton body. No wonder they sank so deep in the mud!

Sand blew over the mud and covered the tracks. In time—millions and millions of years of time—the mud turned to stone and saved this track to tell us that all those years ago a sauropod went by here.

Look! He wasn't alone.
Here are different tracks—
with three pointy claws.
This is bad news.

These are probably the footprints
of an allosaur—
a meat eater, with big jaws
and sharp, curved teeth.
Spying the sauropod,
the allosaur began running after him.
The sauropod looked like a good
meal to him.

Did he ever catch him?
Or did the sauropod get away?
We don't know.
The tracks lead under a big
limestone cliff.
We can't get to them.
Maybe someday we'll find out
how the story ended.

These chase tracks were discovered
near the town of Glen Rose, Texas, in 1938,
by dinosaur expert Roland Bird.
People around there always thought
they were just big holes in the ground.
But when Bird saw them,
he knew right away they were dino tracks,
probably the tracks of a sauropod.
But what kind?
Because of bones found nearby,
scientists think the tracks
were made by a kind of sauropod
known as a brachiosaurid.

Another time when Roland Bird was in Texas,
someone said to him,
"Say, do you want to see some
elephant tracks?"

Bird went with the man
to a ranch near San Antonio.

Let's take a look at what they saw.

There's one problem.
Scientists can analyze rock
to see how old it is.
They could tell that this rock with the tracks
was formed more than 100 million years ago.
There were no elephants then!
So—who made these "elephant tracks?"

The truth is, it was another sauropod.
The track looks different from the others
because it's only the front footprints.
Now wait a minute!
Don't tell me the sauropod was doing
some kind of acrobatic balancing act,
walking on his front feet!
What was going on, anyhow?

Here's a clue . . .
There's also one single sauropod hind footprint.

Have you ever pushed yourself along in
shallow water, "walking" on your hands
along the bottom, with your
body and feet drifting behind you?

That's what the sauropod was doing—
pushing himself along in water with his
front feet, leaving these "elephant tracks" to
puzzle us more than 100 million years later.
He left that one back print when
he was kicking into a turn.

We can see something else.
These prints are not so deep.
That's because his body weight was
being buoyed up by the water.

Let's go.
There are more tracks to follow.
Have you got your flashlight ready?
We're going down 400 feet
into a Colorado coal mine.
How can we find dino tracks down here?

There they are—up on the ceiling!
Big, three-toed footprints.
They're 34 inches long
and 34 inches wide.
But how could the dinosaur walk
underground, upside down?

STATES MINE CO.

This is what happened.
About 80 million years ago
a 25-foot-tall hadrosaur came by here.
Sometimes it walked on all fours.
Other times it stood up
on its hind legs
to browse on conifers and palm trees.
When it wanted to move fast,
it ran on its hind legs.

This one was not hanging around, browsing.
The footprints are 15 feet apart.
That shows it was running fast
through the soft peat.
Why?
We can only guess. . . .

Time passed.
The peat hardened to coal,
leaving these tracks
for us to find.

1.

2.

Of course, the hadrosaur was not
walking underground,
or upside down.
What happened was this:
Over millions of years
sand and sediment
settled over the spot
till the footprints were buried
deeper and deeper.
They were not seen again
till the mine was dug.
And he wasn't walking
upside down either.
What we see here is the bottom
of the prints.

3.

4.

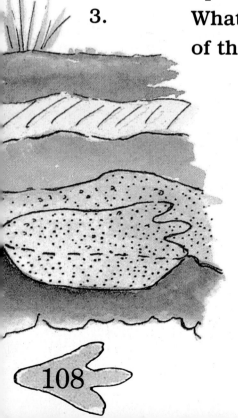

Dino tracks can give us clues
about how dinosaurs lived—
things we wouldn't know
by just looking at their fossilized bones.

The Glen Rose sauropod track
showed that sauropods walked on land.
Before then, paleontologists used to think
that sauropods had to live in water
because their bodies were too heavy
to be supported by feet.

Different sauropod tracks showed something else—that these giant plant-eating dinosaurs often traveled in herds, the way elephants do. The young ones walked in the middle, where they were protected.

Tracks of many Deinonychus are found bunched together. They show that these flesh-eating dinosaurs probably did their hunting in packs.

Tyrannosaurus tracks show us that these big flesh-eaters traveled alone, or in pairs.

111

We used to think all dinosaurs were very sluggish and slow. Dinosaur tracks tell us this was not really so. By studying tracks scientists now have ways to figure out how fast different dinosaurs could run. Some, they say, were pretty speedy.

"Ostrich dinosaurs" could probably run at the rate of 35 miles per hour (mph) or more. This is not as fast as a race horse (45 mph.). But it's faster than an elephant (22 mph).

Tyrannosaurus

Ceratosaurus

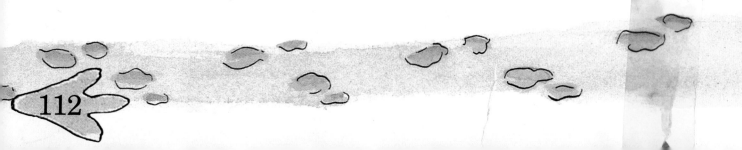

Most scientists think that Tyrannosaurus was slow and clumsy. But some experts now believe it possible that Tyrannosaurus may have been able to run up to 30 mph—at least for a short distance.

Tracks made in Texas by some therapods (two-footed flesh-eaters) showed a running speed of 26 mph.

A hadrosaur track showed a running speed of 16 mph.

Apatosaurus (a kind of sauropod) left a slow-speed track—about 2 to 4 mph.

(This is like the walking speed of a human.) We do not know, though, if this was its top speed. It may have been walking slowly, through mud, or just not been in a hurry.

Apatosaurus

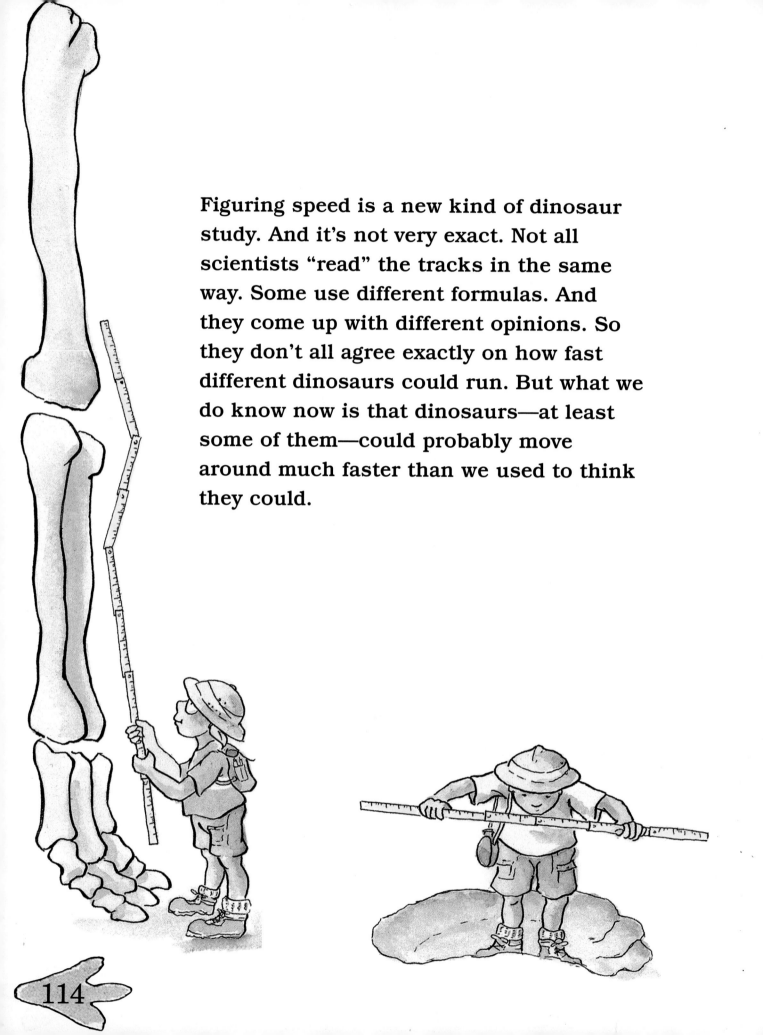

Figuring speed is a new kind of dinosaur study. And it's not very exact. Not all scientists "read" the tracks in the same way. Some use different formulas. And they come up with different opinions. So they don't all agree exactly on how fast different dinosaurs could run. But what we do know now is that dinosaurs—at least some of them—could probably move around much faster than we used to think they could.

Some Facts Scientists Use to Figure Dino Speed

1. Length of dinosaur's **stride**. This is the distance from one footstep to the next step of the same foot. With animals of the same size, a longer stride shows faster speed.

2. **Hip height**. We get this by measuring the length of the leg bones.

3. **Size of foot**. We get this from the footprint.

4. **Width of track**. Usually, a wide track has been made by a slow walker. A narrow track shows faster speed.

wide track

narrow track

Test your own stride:

1. Find a place where your footprints will show (in damp sand).

2. Walk slowly.

3. Walk faster.

4. Run.

5. Measure the stride of each set of footprints.

6. Which prints show the longest stride? (Running). Which prints show the shortest? (Slow walking)

Well, this pith helmet is hot. My canteen is empty. My boots are covered with mud. Let's go home and think about the things we've learned from tracking dinosaurs.

117

LET'S GO DINOSAUR TRACKING!

Meet the Author

Miriam Schlein likes to write about animals that people do not understand. She writes about bats, skunks, pigeons, and porcupines. She also writes fun stories about history. Miriam Schlein has been an author for over forty years!

Meet the Illustrator

Kate Duke When Kate Duke was a child she read and read. She loved books with talking animals that made her laugh. Now she is an author and an illustrator. Her books have many animals in them. One of her favorite characters is a guinea pig!

Theme Connections

Within the Selection

Record your answers to the questions below in the Response Journal section of your Writer's Notebook. In small groups, report the ideas you wrote. Discuss your ideas with the rest of the group. Then choose a person to report your group's answers to the class.

- Where can you go dinosaur tracking?
- What can dinosaur tracks tell scientists that other fossils can't?

Across Selections

- What other selections have you read about fossils?
- How were the characters in this story like the paleontologists in "Dinosaur Fossils"?

Beyond the Selection

- Think about how "Let's Go Dinosaur Tracking" adds to what you know about fossils.
- Add items to the Concept/Question Board about fossils.

hadrosaur

Do you have to be a hero to have courage? Or can courage mean giving an answer in class when you are not sure you are right? Maybe courage can be both of these things. What do you think?

Molly the Brave and Me

Jane O'Connor
illustrated by Sheila Hamanaka

Molly has guts. She has more guts than anybody in the second grade. She can stand at the top of the monkey bars on one foot.

She doesn't mind it when Nicky hides dead water bugs in her desk.

122

And if big kids pick on her, Molly tells them to get lost.

Molly is so brave. I wish I was like her.

Today on the lunch line Molly said to me, "Beth, can you come to our house in the country this weekend? It is lots of fun there."

Wow! I guess Molly really likes me. That made me feel good.

But I have never been away from home. What if I get homesick? What if they eat stuff I don't like?

What if there are lots of wild animals? I was not sure I wanted to go.

I sat at a table with Molly. I said, "Gee, Molly. It sounds neat. Only I don't know if my parents will say yes."

That night Molly's mom called my mom. My mom said yes. So how could I say no? It was all set. Molly's parents were going to pick me up on Saturday morning.

Friday night I packed my stuff. Later my mom tucked me in bed. "I'm scared I'll miss you," I said. "I bet I'll cry all the time. Then Molly will think I'm a big baby. And she won't like me anymore."

My mom hugged me. "You will have fun. And Molly will understand if you are a little homesick." Then my mom kissed me two times. "One kiss is for tonight. The other is for tomorrow night when you will be at Molly's house."

Molly's parents came early the next
morning. I was scared, but I was excited,
too. Most of all I did not want to look like a
wimp around Molly. So I waved good-bye to
my parents and hopped in the back seat.

Molly's dog sat between us. "This is Butch," said Molly. Right away Butch started licking me. I'm kind of scared of big dogs. But did I show it? No way! I acted like I loved getting dog spit all over my face!

By noon we got to Molly's house. It sat all alone at the top of a hill. "This was once a farm," Molly's mom told me. "It's 150 years old."

I like new houses. They haven't had time to get any ghosts. But I didn't say that to Molly's mom.

Right after lunch we went berry picking. That sounded like fun. Then I saw all the beetles on the bushes.

I did not want to touch them. But Molly just swatted them away. So I gave it a try too. "Hey! this is fun," I said. "I have never picked food before."

We ate lots and lots of berries. Red juice got all over my face and hands. I pretended it was blood and I was a vampire.

I chased Molly all around. "You know what?" I told her. "I am really glad that I came to your house."

Later we went looking for wild flowers. That sounded nice and safe to me. We walked all the way down to a stream. A big log lay across the stream.

Molly ran right across it. Boy, what guts! Butch ran across too. I stared at the log. "Aren't there any wild flowers on this side?" I asked.

Molly shook her head. "The best ones are over here. Come on, Beth. Don't be scared. Just walk across—it's easy."

"Okay," I told myself. "Quit acting like a wimp." I started taking tiny steps across the log. Near the end I slipped.

Oof! Down I went. "Are you all right?" Molly asked.

I nodded, but my backside really hurt.

We picked flowers for a while. And when we left, I crawled across the log. Molly didn't tease me. Still I knew I looked like a jerk.

On the way back to the house Butch saw a rabbit and chased it into a field of corn. "Dumb dog!" said Molly. "He will never catch that rabbit. We'd better go and find him."

"Oh, rats!" I thought, but I went in after Molly. We followed the sound of Butch's barks. Boy, was that field big! The corn was way over our heads and it seemed to go on for miles.

At last we spotted Butch. Molly ran and hugged him. Then she pulled me by the arm. "This place is creepy," Molly said. "Let's get out of here."

That was fine with me! But it was not so easy getting out. All the corn looked the same. It was hot and hard to see. Bugs kept flying in our faces. It felt like we were walking around and around in circles.

"Can't Butch help us find the way?" I asked.

Molly shook her head. "Butch can't find his own doghouse."

Then Molly started blinking hard. And her nose got all runny. "Beth," she said. "We're really stuck in here. I'm scared."

Molly scared? I could not believe it! I held her hand. "Don't be scared," I told her, even though I was scared too. "We'll get out of here."

Then I got an idea. "Come on," I told Molly. I started to walk down the space between two rows of corn. I did not make any turns. I stayed in a straight line.

"Pretend this is a long street," I said. "Sooner or later we have to come to the end of it."

And at last we did! Molly and I hugged each other and jumped up and down. Woof! Woof! went Butch. "Hot stuff!" said Molly. "You got us out."

When we got back to Molly's house, her mother said, "Where have you girls been? It is almost time for dinner."

Molly told her parents about following Butch into the corn. Then she put her arm around me.

"I was scared stiff," Molly told them. "But Beth wasn't scared at all. Boy, does she have guts!"

Guts? Me? I couldn't believe my ears!

Dinner was great. We cooked hot dogs on sticks over a fire.

And there was plenty of corn on the cob.
"Oh, no! Not corn!" Molly and I shouted
together. But we each ate three ears anyway.

Right before bed I did get a little homesick. Molly's mom gave me a big hug. That helped.

Then Molly told me I was her best friend. We locked pinkies on it. That helped too.

Maybe Molly was right. Maybe I really am a kid with guts!

Molly the Brave and Me

Meet the Author

Jane O'Connor grew up on the west side of New York City. Since 1979 she has written many children's books, including a cookbook. She used her personal experiences at summer camp to write her first children's book, *Yours Till Niagara Falls, Abby.* She often works with other authors to write stories and nonfiction books.

Meet the Illustrator

Sheila Hamanaka would draw at the many museums she visited. Many ideas have come from memories of favorite places that she visited with her father. Her favorite subject to paint is people because there are so many different types. She likes to illustrate children's books because *"you can do anything you want, any subject."* She lives in the northern part of New York.

Theme Connections

Within the Selection

Writer's Notebook Record your answers to the questions below in the Response Journal section of your Writer's Notebook. In small groups, report the ideas you wrote. Discuss your ideas with the rest of the group. Then choose a person to report your group's answers to the class.

- Why didn't Beth say no when Molly invited her to the country?
- How did Beth find out that she had courage after all?

Across Selections

- Did it take courage for the people in "The Story of Three Whales" to rescue the whales? Why?

Beyond the Selection

- Have you ever needed courage to help you through a new experience? How was it alike or different from Molly's experience?
- How might the story have ended if Beth hadn't been brave and remained calm?
- Add items to the Concept/Question Board about courage.

Courage

Emily Hearn
illustrated by Bo-Kim Louie

Courage is when you're allergic to cats and

your new friend says can you come to her house to play after school and

stay to dinner then maybe go skating and sleep overnight? And,

she adds, you can pet her small kittens! Oh, how you ache to. It

takes courage to say "no" to all that.

Dragons
and Giants

by Arnold Lobel

Frog and Toad were reading a book together. "The people in this book are brave," said Toad. "They fight dragons and giants, and they are never afraid."

"I wonder if we are brave," said Frog. Frog and Toad looked into a mirror.

"We look brave," said Frog.

"Yes, but are we?" asked Toad.

Frog and Toad went outside.

"We can try to climb this mountain," said Frog. "That should tell us if we are brave."

Frog went leaping over rocks, and Toad came puffing up behind him.

They came to a dark cave. A big snake came out of the cave.

"Hello lunch," said the snake when he saw Frog and Toad. He opened his wide mouth. Frog and Toad jumped away. Toad was shaking.

"I am not afraid!" he cried.

They climbed higher, and they heard a
loud noise. Many large stones were rolling
down the mountain.

"It's an avalanche!" cried Toad. Frog and
Toad jumped away. Frog was trembling.

"I am not afraid!" he shouted.

They came to the top of the mountain.
The shadow of a hawk fell over them. Frog
and Toad jumped under a rock. The hawk
flew away.

"We are not afraid!" screamed Frog and Toad at the same time. Then they ran down the mountain very fast. They ran past the place where they saw the avalanche. They ran past the place where they saw the snake. They ran all the way to Toad's house.

"Frog, I am glad to have a brave friend like you," said Toad. He jumped into the bed and pulled the covers over his head.

"And I am happy to know a brave person like you, Toad," said Frog. He jumped into the closet and shut the door.

Toad stayed in the bed, and Frog stayed in the closet.

They stayed there for a long time, just feeling very brave together.

Dragons and Giants

Meet the Author and Illustrator

Arnold Lobel was not big and strong when he was a child. Sometimes the other children would tease him. He would often make up stories to protect himself from the bullies and to amuse his friends. This was good practice for his later career as an author and illustrator.

During summer vacations, he and his family spent time in Vermont. His children caught many frogs and toads. Sometimes they took them home to New York to keep as pets for the year. The following summer, they would return the creatures where they had found them. Arnold Lobel said, *"I loved those little creatures and I think they led to the creation of my two most famous characters, Frog and Toad."*

Theme Connections

Within the Selection

Writer's Notebook   Record your answers to the questions below in the Response Journal section of your Writer's Notebook. In small groups, report the ideas you wrote. Discuss your ideas with the rest of the group. Then choose a person to report your group's answers to the class.

- Frog and Toad said they were not afraid. What do you think?
- Do you think Frog and Toad proved that they are brave? Why?

Across Selections

- How are Frog and Toad like Beth in "Molly the Brave and Me"?

Beyond the Selection

- Have you ever done something to prove that you were brave? What did you do?
- Think about how "Dragons and Giants" adds to what you know about courage.
- Add items to the Concept/Question Board about courage.

Life doesn't frighten me

Maya Angelou
Illustrated by Dara Goldman

Shadow on the wall
Noises down the hall
Life doesn't frighten me at all
Bad dogs barking loud
Big ghosts in a cloud
Life doesn't frighten me at all.

Mean old Mother Goose
Lions on the loose
They don't frighten me at all
Dragons breathing flame
On my counterpane
That doesn't frighten me at all.

I go boo
Make them shoo
I make fun
Way them run
I won't cry
So they fly
I just smile
They go wild
Life doesn't frighten me at all.

158

Tough guys in a fight
All alone at night
Life doesn't frighten me at all.
Panthers in the park
Strangers in the dark
No, they don't frighten me at all.

That new classroom where
Boys all pull my hair
(Kissy little girls
With their hair in curls)
They don't frighten me at all.

Don't show me frogs and snakes
And listen for my scream,
If I'm afraid at all
It's only in my dreams.

I've got a magic charm
That I keep up my sleeve,
I can walk the ocean floor
And never have to breathe.

Life doesn't frighten me at all
Not at all
Not at all
Life doesn't frighten me at all.

The Hole in the Dike

retold by Norma Green

illustrated by Eric Carle

A long time ago, a boy named Peter lived
in Holland. He lived with his mother and
father in a cottage next to a tulip field.
    Peter loved to look at the old windmills
turning slowly.

He loved to look at the sea.
In Holland, the land is very low, and the
sea is very high. The land is kept safe and
dry by high, strong walls called dikes.

One day Peter went to visit a friend who
lived by the seaside.

As he started for home, he saw that the sun
was setting and the sky was growing dark. "I
must hurry or I shall be late for supper," said
Peter.

"Take the short-cut along the top of the
dike," his friend said.

They waved good-bye.

Peter wheeled his bike to the road on top
of the dike. It had rained for several days,
and the water looked higher than usual.

Peter thought, "It's lucky that the dikes are
high and strong. Without these dikes, the land
would be flooded and everything would be
washed away."

Suddenly he heard a soft, gurgling noise.
He saw a small stream of water trickling
through a hole in the dike below.

Peter got off his bike to see what was wrong.

He couldn't believe his eyes. There in the
big strong dike was a leak!

164

Peter slid down to the bottom of the dike.
He put his finger in the hole to keep the
water from coming through.

He looked around for help, but he could
not see anyone on the road. He shouted.
Maybe someone in the nearby field would
hear him, he thought.

Only his echo answered. Everyone had
gone home.

Peter knew that if he let the water leak
through the hole in the dike, the hole would
get bigger and bigger. Then the sea would
come gushing through. The fields and the
houses and the windmills would all be flooded.

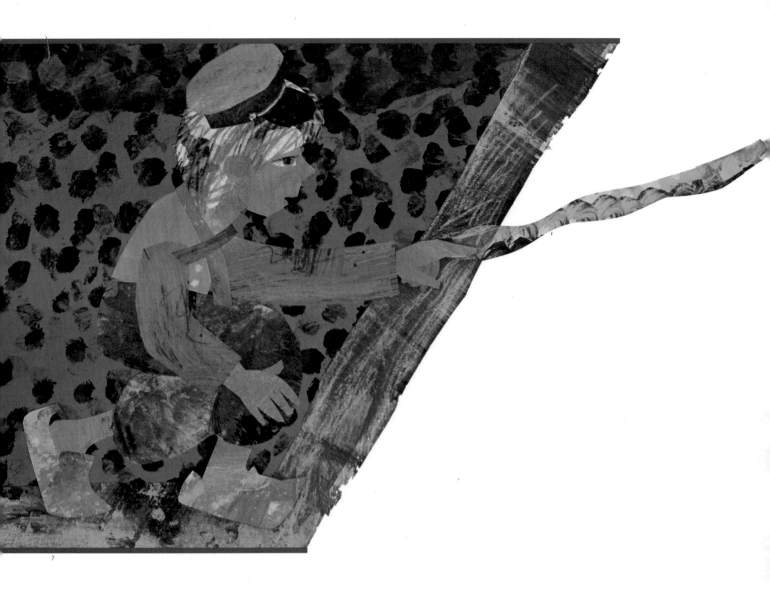

Peter looked around for something to plug
up the leak so he could go to the village
for help.

He put a stone in the hole, then a stick. But
the stone and the stick were washed away
by the water.

Peter had to stay there alone. He had to use all his strength to keep the water out.

From time to time he called for help. But no one heard him.

All night long Peter kept his finger in the dike.

His fingers grew cold and numb. He wanted to sleep, but he couldn't give up.

At last, early in the morning, Peter heard a welcome sound. Someone was coming! It was the milk cart rumbling down the road.

Peter shouted for help. The milkman was surprised to hear someone near that road so early in the morning. He stopped and looked around.

"Help!!" Peter shouted. "Here I am, at the bottom of the dike. There's a leak in the dike. Help! Help!"

The man saw Peter and hurried down to him. Peter showed him the leak and the little stream of water coming through.

Peter asked the milkman to hurry to the village. "Tell the people. Ask them to send some men to repair the dike right away!"

The milkman went as fast as he could. Peter had to stay with his finger in the dike.

At last the men from the village came. They set to work to repair the leak.

All the people thanked Peter. They carried him on their shoulders, shouting, "Make way for the hero of Holland! The brave boy who saved our land!"

But Peter did not think of himself as a
hero. He had done what he thought was
right. He was glad that he could do
something for the country he loved so
much.

The Hole in the Dike

Meet the Author

Norma Green says that more than a hundred years ago, an American woman named Mary Mapes Dodge told this story of the dike to her children, making it up as she went along. It was first published in her book *Hans Brinker or the Silver Skates*. The story became so famous that the Dutch people put up a statue of Peter in a little town called Spaarndam.

Green said, *"I felt there was a need today for young people to read about courage and pride in country. This story seemed to be a way of passing on these messages in a memorable fantasy."*

Meet the Illustrator

Eric Carle was born in New York. When he was six, his parents moved to Germany. After finishing art school in Germany, he moved back to the United States. He worked for a newspaper, the army, and an advertising agency before working as an illustrator full time. His books are often full of surprises. His books sometimes have pages with holes, flaps to look behind, uneven pages, and foldouts. He often hides the initials or names of his two children, Cirsten and Rolf, in his illustrations.

Theme Connections

Within the Selection

 Writer's Notebook Record your answers to the questions below in the Response Journal section of your Writer's Notebook. In small groups, report the ideas you wrote. Discuss your ideas with the rest of the group. Then choose a person to report your group's answers to the class.

- How did Peter find the courage to plug the hole in the dike?
- Why did the people think Peter was a brave hero?

Across Selections

- What other stories have you read that show courage?
- The people in "The Hole in the Dike" called Peter a hero. Who might Molly have called a hero in "Molly the Brave and Me"? Why?

Beyond the Selection

- Think about how "The Hole in the Dike" adds to what you know about courage.
- Add items to the Concept/Question Board about courage.

Warrior Chief, warriors, and attendants. 16th–17th century. **Bini people, from the palace in Benin City, Nigeria.** Brass plaque. The Metropolitan Museum of Art, New York.

Lake Spirit. 1988. **Dale De Armond.**
Wood engraving on paper. 6 × 5 in.
The National Museum of Women in the
Arts, Washington, D.C.

The Life-Line. 1884. **Winslow Homer.** Oil on canvas.
Philadelphia Museum of Art.

A Picture Book of
Martin Luther King, Jr.

David A. Adler

illustrated by Robert Casilla

Martin Luther King, Jr. was one of America's great leaders. He was a powerful speaker, and he spoke out against laws which kept black people out of many schools and jobs. He led protests and marches demanding fair laws for all people.

Martin Luther King, Jr. was born on January 15, 1929 in Atlanta, Georgia. Martin's father was a pastor. His mother had been a teacher. Martin had an older sister, Willie Christine, and a younger brother, Alfred Daniel.

Young Martin liked to play baseball, football, and basketball. He liked to ride his bicycle and to sing. He often sang in his father's church.

Martin (center) with his brother Alfred Daniel (left) and his sister Willie Christine (right)

Young Martin played in his backyard with his friends. One day he was told that two of his friends would no longer play with him, because they were white and he was black.

Martin cried. He didn't understand why the color of his skin should matter to anyone.

Martin's mother told him that many years ago black people were brought in chains to America and sold as slaves. She told him that long before Martin was born the slaves had been set free. However, there were still some people who did not treat black people fairly.

In Atlanta, where Martin lived, and elsewhere in the United States, there were "White Only" signs. Black people were not allowed in some parks, pools, hotels, restaurants and even schools. Blacks were kept out of many jobs.

Martin learned to read at home before he was old enough to start school. All through his childhood, he read books about black leaders.

Frederick Douglass

Harriet Tubman

George Washington Carver

Martin was a good student. He finished high school two years early and was just fifteen when he entered Morehouse College in Atlanta. At college Martin decided to become a minister.

After Martin was graduated from Morehouse, he studied for a doctorate at Boston University. While he was there he met Coretta Scott. She was studying music. They fell in love and married.

In 1954 Martin Luther King, Jr. began his first job as a pastor in Montgomery, Alabama. The next year Rosa Parks, a black woman, was arrested in Montgomery. She had been sitting just behind the "White Only" section on the bus. When all the seats in that section were taken, the driver told her to get up so a white man could have her seat. Rosa Parks refused.

Dr. Martin Luther King, Jr. led a protest. Blacks throughout the city refused to ride the buses. Dr. King said, "There comes a time when people get tired of being kicked about."

One night, while Dr. King was at a meeting, someone threw a bomb into his house.

Martin's followers were angry. They wanted to fight. Martin told them to go home peacefully. "We must love our white brothers," he said. "We must meet hate with love."

The bus protest lasted almost a year. When it ended there were no more "White Only" sections on buses.

Dr. King decided to move back to Atlanta in 1960. There, he continued to lead peaceful protests against "White Only" waiting rooms, lunch counters and rest rooms. He led many marches for freedom.

In 1963 Dr. King led the biggest march of all—the March on Washington. More than two hundred thousand black and white people followed him. "I have a dream," he said in his speech. "I have a dream that my four children will one day live in a nation where they will not be judged by the color of their skin but by the content of their character."

The next year in 1964, Dr. King was awarded one of the greatest honors any person can win, the Nobel Peace Prize.

The country was changing. New laws were passed. Blacks could go to the same schools as whites. They could go to the same stores, restaurants and hotels. "White Only" signs were against the law.

Dr. King told his followers to protest peacefully. But there were some riots and some violence.

Then, in April 1968, Dr. King went to Memphis, Tennessee. He planned to march so black and white garbage workers would get the same pay for the same work.

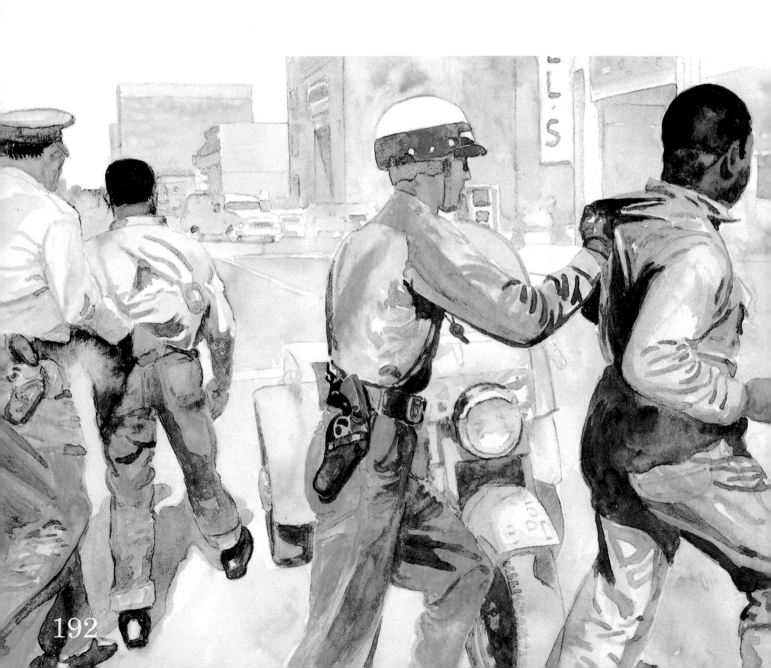

On April 4 in Memphis, Dr. King stood outside his motel room. Another man, James Earl Ray, was hiding nearby. He pointed a rifle at Dr. King. He fired the gun. An hour later Dr. King was dead.

Martin Luther King, Jr. dreamed of a world free of hate, prejudice and violence. Carved on the stone which marks his grave are the words, "I'm free at last."

A Picture Book of
Martin Luther King, Jr.

Meet the Author

David Adler's parents encouraged all six of their children to read and develop their own talents. He was known for his artistic ability and he would often tell stories to his brothers and sisters.

He was a math teacher, a cartoonist, and an arts and crafts teacher before he became a writer. He wrote his first children's book while he was a math teacher. By watching and listening to other people, he gets many ideas for his stories.

Meet the Illustrator

Robert Casilla was born in Jersey City, New Jersey. He began illustrating after graduating from the School of Visual Arts. He said, *"I find great rewards and satisfaction in illustrating for children."*

He has illustrated ten other biographies written by David Adler. When he illustrates a biography, he first tries to learn a lot about the person. Knowing the person very well helps him when he works on the art.

Theme Connections

Within the Selection

Writer's Notebook — Record your answers to the questions below in the Response Journal section of your Writer's Notebook. In small groups, report the ideas you wrote. Discuss your ideas with the rest of the group. Then choose a person to report your group's answers to the class.

- What did Martin Luther King, Jr. do in his life that was brave?
- Why was Martin Luther King, Jr. willing to put himself in danger to help others?

Across Selections

- The other stories in this unit so far have been fictional. How is "A Picture Book of Martin Luther King, Jr." different?
- What did Peter in "The Hole in the Dike" have in common with Martin Luther King, Jr.?

Beyond the Selection

- Think about how "A Picture Book of Martin Luther King, Jr." adds to what you know about courage.
- Add items to the Concept/Question Board about courage.

The Empty Pot

by Demi

A long time ago in China there was a boy named Ping who loved flowers. Anything he planted burst into bloom. Up came flowers, bushes, and even big fruit trees, as if by magic!

Everyone in the kingdom loved flowers too. They planted them everywhere, and the air smelled like perfume.

196

The Emperor loved birds and animals, but flowers most of all, and he tended his own garden every day. But the Emperor was very old. He needed to choose a successor to the throne.

Who would his successor be? And how would the Emperor choose? Because the Emperor loved flowers so much, he decided to let the flowers choose.

The next day a proclamation was issued:
All the children in the land were to come to
the palace. There they would be given special
flower seeds by the Emperor. "Whoever can
show me their best in a year's time," he said,
"will succeed me to the throne."

This news created great excitement throughout the land! Children from all over the country swarmed to the palace to get their flower seeds. All the parents wanted their children to be chosen Emperor, and all the children hoped they would be chosen too!

When Ping received his seed from the Emperor, he was the happiest child of all. He was sure he could grow the most beautiful flower.

Ping filled a flowerpot with rich soil. He planted the seed in it very carefully.

He watered it every day. He couldn't wait to see it sprout, grow, and blossom into a beautiful flower!

Day after day passed, but nothing grew in his pot.

Ping was very worried. He put new soil into a bigger pot. Then he transferred the seed into the rich black soil.

Another two months he waited. Still nothing happened.

By and by the whole year passed.

Spring came, and all the children put on their best clothes to greet the Emperor.

They rushed to the palace with their beautiful flowers, eagerly hoping to be chosen.

Ping was ashamed of his empty pot. He thought the other children would laugh at him because for once he couldn't get a flower to grow.

His clever friend ran by, holding a great big plant. "Ping!" he said. "You're not really going to the Emperor with an empty pot, are you? Couldn't you grow a great big flower like mine?"

"I've grown lots of flowers better than yours," Ping said. "It's just this seed that won't grow."

Ping's father overheard this and said, "You did your best, and your best is good enough to present to the Emperor."

Holding the empty pot in his hands, Ping went straight away to the palace.

The Emperor was looking at the flowers
slowly, one by one.

How beautiful all the flowers were!

But the Emperor was frowning and did not
say a word.

Finally he came to Ping. Ping hung his
head in shame, expecting to be punished.

The Emperor asked him, "Why did you bring an empty pot?"

Ping started to cry and replied, "I planted the seed you gave me and I watered it every day, but it didn't sprout. I put it in a better pot with better soil, but still it didn't sprout! I tended it all year long, but nothing grew. So today I had to bring an empty pot without a flower. It was the best I could do."

When the Emperor heard these words, a smile slowly spread over his face, and he put his arm around Ping. Then he exclaimed to one and all, "I have found him! I have found the one person worthy of being Emperor!

"Where you got your seeds from, I do not know. For the seeds I gave you had all been cooked. So it was impossible for any of them to grow.

"I admire Ping's great courage to appear before me with the empty truth, and now I reward him with my entire kingdom and make him Emperor of all the land!"

The Empty Pot

Meet the Author and Illustrator

Charlotte Dumaresq Hunt uses her childhood nickname, Demi, as her pen name. She studied art in several schools, but much of her learning took place as she traveled. She has been to faraway places such as Brazil, India, and China. Some of the things she learned and saw while in China are seen in "The Empty Pot."

She has not limited her art to children's books. Many of her paintings and prints hang in museums in the United States and India. She has also painted wall murals in Mexico and the dome of a church in California.

Theme Connections

Within the Selection

Writer's Notebook Record your answers to the questions below in the Response Journal section of your Writer's Notebook. In small groups, report the ideas you wrote. Discuss your ideas with the rest of the group. Then choose a person to report your group's answers to the class.

- Ping was ashamed of his empty pot. Why did he present it to the Emperor anyway?
- How did the Emperor know that Ping deserved to be Emperor?

Across Selections

- Were you surprised by the ending? Why? Did any other stories that we've read surprise you at the end? Explain.
- How might the story have been different had Ping not been honest?

Beyond the Selection

- Have you ever needed courage when you didn't think your best was good enough? What happened?
- Think about how "The Empty Pot" adds to what you know about courage.
- Add items to the Concept/Question Board about courage.

Focus Questions Why do we need to have the courage to stand up to our fears? Have you ever had a fear of standing up in front of an audience? How did you overcome this fear?

Brave as a Mountain Lion

Ann Herbert Scott
illustrated by Glo Coalson

It was snowing hard. Pressing his face against the cold glass of the living room window, Spider could barely see his father's horses crowding against the fence. Soon the reservation would be covered with darkness.

Spider shivered. Any other night he would have been hoping his father would reach home before the snow drifted too high to push through. But tonight was different. Tonight he dreaded his father's coming.

In his pocket Spider could feel two pieces of paper from school. One he wanted to show his father. One he didn't. Not tonight. Not ever.

Beside him on the couch his sister Winona was playing with her doll. Lucky kid, thought Spider. Winona was too little to worry about anything, especially school.

Just then Spider saw the blinking red lights
of the snowplow clearing the road beside their
house. Right behind came his father's new
blue pickup. Spider sighed. At least Dad was
home safe. Now the trouble would begin!

Winona ran to the back door. But Spider stayed on the couch, waiting. From the kitchen he could smell dinner cooking. His favorite, deer meat. But tonight he didn't even feel like eating. Soon he heard the sound of his father and his brother Will stomping the snow from their boots.

Spider's father came in with an armful of mail from the post office. He hung up his hat and jacket on the pegs by the kitchen and stretched out in his favorite chair.

"So what did you do in school today?" he asked Spider.

"Not much," said Spider, feeling his pocket.

"Did you bring home any papers?"

Spider nodded. How did his father always know?

"Let's take a look," said his father.

Spider took the first paper from his pocket. "Here's the good one," he said.

"Spelling one hundred percent. Every word correct. Good for you, son."

"But, Dad, I'm in trouble." Spider shoved the other paper into his father's hand. "The teacher wants me to be in the big school spelling bee."

Spider's father read out loud: "Dear Parent, I am pleased to inform you that your son Spider has qualified for the school spelling bee, which will be held next Thursday night. We hope you and your family will attend."

Spider's mother and grandmother came in from the kitchen with the platter of deer meat and bowls of beans and corn for dinner. "That's a good report, Little Brother," his grandmother said, smiling.

"But I won't do it," said Spider.

"Why not?" asked Will.

"I'm too afraid," said Spider.

"But you're a brave boy," said his father. "Why are you afraid?"

"Dad," said Spider, "you have to stand high up on the stage in the gym and all the people look at you. I'm afraid my legs would freeze together and I wouldn't be able to walk. And if I did get up there, no sound would come out when I opened my mouth. It's too scary."

"Oh, I see," said his father.

Spider's mother put her hand on his shoulder. "You must be hungry. Let's eat."

After dinner Spider sat by the wood stove doing his homework. "Dad, were you ever in a spelling bee?" he asked.

"As a matter of fact, I was."

"Were you scared?"

"I was very scared. I didn't even want to do it. But then my father told me to pretend I was a brave animal, the strongest, bravest animal I could think of. Then I wasn't afraid anymore."

Later, Spider sat up in bed thinking of animals who weren't afraid of anything. Above his head hung the picture of a mountain lion his dad had painted for him. How about a mountain lion, the King of the Beasts?

Spider took his flashlight from under his pillow and shined its beam on the face of the great wild creature. "Brave as a mountain lion," he said to himself in a loud, strong voice.

"Brave as a mountain lion," he repeated in his mind as he was falling asleep.

"I'll try to be brave as a mountain lion," he whispered to his father the next morning as he brushed his hair for school.

At recess the next day Spider peeked into the gymnasium. The huge room was empty. He looked up at the mural painting of the western Shoshone people of long ago. They were brave hunters of deer and antelope and elk, just as his father and his uncles were today.

At the far end of the gym was the scoreboard with the school's emblem, the eagle. Every Saturday in the winter Spider and his whole family came to cheer for Will and the basketball team. Those players weren't afraid of anything.

Then Spider stared up at the stage. That's where the spellers would stand. He could feel his throat tighten and hear his heart thumping, bumpity-bumpity-bumpity-bump. How could he ever get up there in front of all the people? Spider ran outside, slamming the gym door behind him.

That afternoon it was still snowing. At home Spider found his grandmother beading a hatband for his father's birthday. Spider watched her dip her needle into the bowls of red and black and white beads.

"Grandma, were you ever in a spelling bee?"

"No, I never was," his grandmother answered. "Are you thinking much about it?"

"All the time," said Spider.

"What's the worst part?"

"Being up on the stage with all the people looking at you."

"Oh, that's easy," said his grandmother. "You can be clever. Clever as a coyote. The coyote always has some trick to help him out of trouble. When you're up there on the stage, you don't have to look at the people. You can turn your back on them and pretend they aren't even there."

In bed that night Spider pulled the covers over his head. "Brave as a mountain lion, clever as a coyote," he kept repeating to himself as he fell asleep.

The next morning Spider scraped a peephole in the ice on his bedroom window. He couldn't see the far mountains for the swirling snow. He smiled as he packed his book bag. If it kept snowing like this, maybe the principal would close school tomorrow.

In class that day all everybody could talk about was the spelling bee. "Can we count on you, Spider?" asked Miss Phillips, his teacher.

Spider shook his head. "Maybe," he said. "I haven't made up my mind."

"You'd better make up your mind soon," said Miss Phillips. "The spelling bee is tomorrow night."

After lunch Spider walked by the gym door, but this time he didn't open it. He didn't have to. He remembered just how everything looked. Scary. When he thought about it, a shiver went all the way down his spine.

By the afternoon the snow had piled in drifts higher than Spider's head. Spider got a bowl of popcorn and went to the carport to watch Will shoot baskets. Time after time the ball slipped through the net. Will almost never missed.

"How about some popcorn for me?" Will asked his little brother. Spider brought back another bowl from the kitchen.

"Are you practicing for the spelling bee?" asked Will.

"I've decided not to be in it," said Spider. "I'm going to be brave when I'm bigger."

Will nodded. "I remember those spelling bees."

"Were you afraid?" asked Spider.

"I was scared silly," said Will. "I was so scared I was afraid I'd wet my pants. Then I learned the secret."

"What's the secret?" asked Spider.

"To be silent."

"Silent?" asked Spider. "What does that do?"

"It keeps you cool. When I have a hard shot to make and the whole team depends on me, that's when I get very silent."

Spider didn't say anything. He just watched his brother shooting one basket after another. Then he saw her. High above the shelves of paint and livestock medicines was a tiny insect. It was his old friend, Little Spider, dangling on a long strand as she spun a new part of her web. She was silent. Silent as the moon.

Spider laughed. How could he have forgotten! Grandmother often told him how when he was a baby in his cradle board he used to watch for hours while a little spider spun her web above his head. She had been his first friend. Ever since, his family had called him Spider.

Taking the stepladder, Spider climbed up close so he could watch the tiny creature. How brave she was, dropping down into space with nothing to hang onto. And how clever, weaving a web out of nothing but her own secret self. "Say something," he whispered.

The little insect was silent. But Spider felt she was talking to him in her own mysterious way. "Listen to your spirit," she seemed to say. "Listen to your spirit and you'll never be afraid."

The next morning the snow had stopped. Outside Spider's window icicles glistened in the sun. No chance of school being closed today.

"Brave as a mountain lion, clever as a coyote, silent as a spider," Spider thought to himself as he buttoned his vest.

Winona pushed open the door. "Are you going to do it?"

"I'm going to do it," Spider answered.

That night all the family came, his grandmother who lived with them and his other grandparents and his father and his mother and three aunts and two uncles and Will and Winona and lots of their cousins. Three of his cousins were going to be in the spelling bee, too.

Brave as a mountain lion, Spider climbed up the steps to the stage. Clever as a coyote, he turned his back so he wouldn't see the rows of people down below. Silently, he listened to his spirit. Bumpity-bump-bump went his heart.

All the best spellers in his class were up there on the stage, standing in a line. The principal gave them the words, one by one.

At first the words were easy. "Yellow," said the principal. "I have a yellow dog."

Spider kept his eyes on the principal's face. "Yellow," said Spider. "Y-e-l-l-o-w. Yellow."

"Correct," said the principal.

Then the words got a little harder. "February," said the principal. "Soon it will be February." It was Spider's turn again.

"February," said Spider, remembering the *r*. "Capital f-e-b-r-u-a-r-y. February."

"Correct," said the principal.

Finally there were only two spellers left standing—Spider and Elsie, a girl from the other side of the reservation.

"Terrific," said the principal. "We have a terrific basketball team."

"Terrific," said Spider, taking a big breath. "T-e-r-r-i-f-f-i-c. Terrific."

"Incorrect," said the principal. Then she turned to Elsie. "Terrific. We have a terrific basketball team."

"Terrific," said Elsie. "T-e-r-r-i-f-i-c. Terrific."

"Correct," said the principal. "Let's give a hand to our two winners from Miss Phillips' class: Elsie in first place and Spider in second place."

It was over! Spider climbed down the steps and found the rows where his family were sitting. Spider's father shook his hand and Will slapped him on the back. "You did it!" his mother said proudly. "You stood right up there in front of everybody!"

"It was easy," said Spider.

"You were brave," said his father. "Brave as a mountain lion."

"And clever," said his grandmother. "Clever as a coyote."

I wasn't even afraid, Spider thought. I listened to my spirit. "But now I'm hungry," he told his family. "Hungry as a bear. Let's all go home and eat."

Brave as a Mountain Lion

Meet the Author

Ann Herbert Scott often becomes familiar with the people and places she writes about. As she writes, she pictures each scene in her mind. She also talks a lot with children to see what they think about her ideas. When speaking about this story, she said, *"The story idea came directly from a boy who was confronted by an everyday challenge to his courage: his fear of standing up before an audience as part of the annual school spelling bee."*

Meet the Illustrator

Glo Coalson has always loved art and the out-of-doors. After a friend suggested that she illustrate books, she wrote and illustrated her first book. It was created from Eskimo folktales that she had collected while in Alaska. Since then, she has illustrated over 20 children's books. She uses watercolor, pastels, and ink to create her illustrations.

Theme Connections

Within the Selection

Writer's Notebook Record your answers to the questions below in the Response Journal section of your Writer's Notebook. In small groups, report the ideas you wrote. Discuss your ideas with the rest of the group. Then choose a person to report your group's answers to the class.

- Why was Spider afraid of being in the spelling bee?

- How was Spider able to overcome his fear of being in the spelling bee?

Across Selections

- Compare how Spider overcame his fear of the spelling bee and how Beth in "Molly the Brave and Me" overcame her fears.

- What was Ping in "The Empty Pot" afraid of? What was Spider afraid of? How were their fears alike or different?

Beyond the Selection

- When have you been afraid to do something? What helped you have courage?

- Think about how "Brave as a Mountain Lion" adds to what you know about courage.

- Add items to the Concept/Question Board about courage.

Our Country and Its People

Many people in this country came from faraway countries to live here. Where did they come from? Why did they come? Did your family come from far away? Meet some of these people and find out their stories.

The First Americans

Jane Werner Watson
illustrated by Troy Howell

PEOPLE OF THE PLAINS

Long years ago in all our wide land there were no cities. There were no railways or roads. There were no horses or wheels. But there were people living here.

The people lived in small groups scattered over the land. Some wandered across the wide grassy plains hunting for food. They carried their homes—called *tepees*—with them. The women and girls of these groups could set up the tepees quickly.

The men hunted wild buffalo. The people ate
the meat of the buffalo. They wore its hide
for clothing. They covered their tepees with
buffalo hide. The men made tools from buffalo
bones. No wonder these nations came to be
known as the people of the buffalo!

Winters were hard on the plains. The people
set up camps close to rivers. Some heaped
earth around the bottom of their tepees.
Others built lodges of earth to keep out the
winter winds. Often there was not much food.

Boys were sent out alone at night to fetch water. Or they spent days and nights alone without food or water to test their bravery. Boys of the plains nations wanted to grow up to be good hunters and warriors.

They learned to make war whistles, war clubs, and bows and arrows. They also learned to shape bowls for pipes from stone and to make stems from wood. A boy started work as a moccasin-bearer or as a servant to a warrior. Then he became a water-carrier.

After that he scouted for herds of buffalo and kept an eye out for enemies. If he was a good scout he became a warrior. The best warrior became the chief.

For play, the boys wrestled or rolled small hoops
with spears. They spun tops and played stick ball.
Their balls were made of deer or buffalo hair
wrapped in strips of hide.

Girls played house with toy tepees or carried
puppies on their backs instead of baby dolls.
And they helped their mothers.

PEOPLE OF THE EASTERN WOODLANDS

East of the Mississippi River most of the land was covered with great forests. Many animals lived in the forests—bear and woodland buffalo and deer. The men of the woodland nations hunted these animals for food for their families.

They also hunted smaller animals—rabbit, beaver, opossum, squirrel, and wild turkey. Boys of these nations learned to move silently through the forest so they could be good hunters. The men and boys also cleared trees and burned bushes.

In these clearings, the women and girls raised corn and beans and squash. They also gathered fruits and nuts and grass seeds and bulbs that were good to eat. In the fall, children gathered walnuts, hickory nuts, and acorns in the woods.

The woodland people liked to live together in villages. In summer many of them moved to summer homes near a lake or stream. They caught fish, turtles, and shellfish. When water birds flew south in the fall, the men caught some of them for food. Usually there was plenty to eat in the woods.

Homes were made of poles covered with
bark or mud or grass mats to keep out the
harsh weather. Some of them were round.
They were called *wigwams* or *wickiups*.
Other nations built long houses in which
many families lived together.

Each family had its own cooking-fire and a
space for a sleeping-shelf. In the cold winters
people had more time to work indoors. They
made fur robes and leggings and moccasins
trimmed with porcupine quills. They made
smoking pipes
and tools, and
decorations of
shell beads.

The women wove baskets out of grass and made boxes and pots of birchbark. Canoes were often made of birchbark, too.

While the families worked, the old people told stories—about the Great Spirit who watched over them from the sky, about the Sun which gave them life, about the Thunderbird who roared from the clouds during storms and the animals which gave them food—and about the heroes of their people.

Some nations made mounds of earth in the shape of snakes, eagles, wildcats, and other animals for which they had special respect. Grass grew over these mounds and some can still be seen today.

Paths led through the woodlands. Sometimes people of other nations came along those paths to trade furs, grain, or hard stone for arrow points. Many of the nations used strings of shell beads called *wampum* to pay for things they bought.

Nations spoke different languages. But they could speak together in sign language. Some Native Americans in the woodlands had fur and wild rice to trade. They did not raise crops. They were hunters and fishermen.

In the snowy winters they walked over the thick, soft snow on snowshoes. They pulled their wares on toboggans. Suits of furry hides kept them warm.

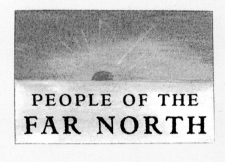

PEOPLE OF THE
FAR NORTH

Noth of the woods, on the icy treeless plains, or *tundra*, other hunters and fishermen lived. They went to sea in skin boats to hunt whale, seal, and fish. On land they traveled in sleds pulled by husky dogs.

There were no trees to give them poles or bark for their homes. So they made houses of snow or chunks of earth rounded at the top over rafters of curved whale bone.

In the long dark winters they sat on their sleeping-shelves inside their warm sod or snow houses. They burned whale blubber for light. Often they did not have much food.

The women and girls worked at softening hide for clothing by chewing it. The men and boys carved tools and decorations from stone, ivory, or bone. And the old people told stories.

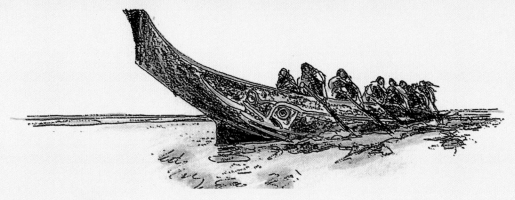

PEOPLE OF THE NORTHWEST COAST

South of the icy tundra, near the Pacific Ocean, deep forests grew. Nations in these forests fished and gathered shellfish from the sea. In the spring they went out in big canoes to hunt giant gray whales.

In the summer the woods gave them berries and fruit. This rich land could feed many families, so people lived in large villages. In the rainy, stormy winters they lived in the shelter of the forests. In spring and summer they paddled their canoes down the coast to summer homes.

They built sturdy wooden houses with posts carved from soft, tall cedar trees. Their canoes were made from cedar logs. And they carved tall poles into the shapes of the animals their families felt related to—deer, bear, turtle, beaver, or eagle.

Many village chiefs and others of these northwest coast nations became rich and powerful. They took pride in having gift-giving parties called *potlaches*. Many other nations also had ceremonies at which they gave gifts of blankets, shawls, baskets, and beadwork. The gifts honored those who got them. They also showed how rich the giver was. Sometimes in one great party a rich man of the northwest coast gave away all he owned! Of course he would soon be invited to someone else's potlach and be given fine gifts in return.

Parties, festivals, music, and dancing were very important to these people of long ago. At the center of almost any village was an open space for dancing. All year there were sun dances, rain dances, corn dances, deer dances, harvest dances, and winter dances.

Every nation had its own special dances. There were special dances to honor young people, both boys and girls, as they grew up.

Often dancers wore costumes. They wore masks to honor a spirit or god. And as a man danced, he seemed to become that spirit. To make music, people beat on painted drums, shook rattles made of dry gourds, and blew into whistles or pipes. Some of the best dances were those of the southwest nations who lived in bare, dry country where it was often very hot.

PEOPLE OF THE SOUTHWEST

Some of the people of the southwest made simple shelters of thin posts or logs covered with brush or clay. But many nations built towns of high-piled houses made of stone or sun-dried brick.

Usually the town was built on top of a cliff or into the side of one, for protection. It was often a long climb to the town's small fields. There was little rain. Water for the corn, beans, and squash had to be brought from streams and pools by digging ditches.

Small boys and girls had long walks, too, taking the family flocks to pasture. These children of long ago had to learn to live with heat and cold, rain, snow, and hunger.

If sickness came, a medicine man was called. He brought herbs to cure the sickness or he called on good spirits to help. A sand painting could bring the spirits.

People of long ago lived close to the spirits of the earth and air and sea and sky. They believed that the land and waters belonged to everyone—to use and to enjoy—and to pass on to their children.

It was over five hundred years ago when sailing ships from Europe started to cross the ocean to this wide land. People of Europe saw the deep forests, the swift rivers, the grassy clearings. They liked what they saw and wanted it for themselves.

More and more of them came, bringing horses, wheels, guns, and many new ways of living. Since then life has never been the same for the nations of the first Americans.

The First Americans

Meet the Author

Jane Werner Watson has written for children for many years. Sometimes when she writes books she uses different names. That is called using a pseudonym. One of her pseudonyms is Elsa Ruth Nast. Jane Werner Watson loves to travel to far away places. She once lived in India!

Meet the Illustrator

Troy Howell is a freelance illustrator of children's books and magazines, including *Cricket*. He has worked on new editions of *Heidi*, *The Adventures of Pinocchio*, and *The Secret Garden*.

Theme Connections

Within the Selection

Writer's Notebook Record your answers to the questions below in the Response Journal section of your Writer's Notebook. In small groups, report the ideas you wrote. Discuss your ideas with the rest of the group. Then choose a person to report your group's answers to the class.

- How were the houses that the people of the Far North built different from the houses that the people of the Northwest Coast built? How did the environment in which they lived affect the kind of houses they built?
- What is a wampum, and what was it used for? What kinds of things did the people of the Eastern Woodlands trade?

Across Selections

- Name some ways that you think the Native Americans showed bravery.

Beyond the Selection

- How was life for the first Americans different from life in our country today? How was it similar?
- Add items to the Concept/Question Board about our country and its people.

New Hope

by Henri Sorensen

Jimmy loved to visit Grandpa. He loved the old-fashioned ice-cream store in New Hope, where Grandpa lived. He loved the recycling dump. And he especially loved the statue in the park. "Who is that man?" Jimmy always asked. And every time, Grandpa told him the same wonderful story.

"That's Lars Jensen," Grandpa began.
"Over one hundred years ago, in 1885,
Lars sailed to this country from Denmark.
He brought his wife, Karen, and their two
children, Peter and Mathilde, to start a new
life in America.

"When they landed in New York, they took a train to Minnesota. There Lars bought a wagon, two horses, a hunting rifle, tools, a tent, several bags of seeds, and plenty of food for the trip. Then he and Karen and Peter and Mathilde began the last part of their long journey. On narrow trails, they traveled through forests and forded rivers and crossed the wide plains.

"Sometimes they joined up with other travelers and Peter and Mathilde fell asleep to tales of Sitting Bull told around the campfire. One night a yellow dog appeared at the campsite. 'He must have followed us from the town we passed through this morning,' said Karen. 'Well, we can't take him back now,' said Lars. So Peter and Mathilde adopted him. They named him Fido.

"One day, just as they came to a river, one of the axles on their wagon broke. Lars took off his hat and scratched his head. Fish were jumping in the river. A doe and her fawn stood at the edge of the forest. *'Pokkers!'* said Lars. 'This looks like a good place. Let's stop here.'

"By the time the first snow fell, they had planted and harvested their first crop and built a small cabin for themselves and a shed for their horses. Each morning after checking their traps, Lars and Peter worked on the fence until Karen called them in for hot stew and bread.

"The following spring, while Karen and Mathilde worked in the garden, Lars and Peter built a small ferry. All that summer Lars ferried people and wagons across the river. Business was brisk—Lars's ferry was the only way to cross the river for miles.

"One day a blacksmith named Franz arrived. A busy ferry landing would bring lots of business, so instead of crossing the river, he stayed to build a forge.

"Soon lumbermen arrived to harvest the rich forests and farmers began to clear the land for their crops. 'All these people need a general store,' said Lars, so he traveled several days to the nearest big town to buy rope and shoes and nails and fabric and all the other things he knew the people would need. He named his shop the New Hope General Store.

"As the years passed, more and more people came to the village by the river. The old slow-moving ferry was replaced by a wooden bridge. Now that crossing the river was so easy, the stage coach began to stop at the New Hope General Store. One day a traveler named Saul got off the stage and stayed. Three months later he opened the New Hope Hotel.

"New Hope became a busy, bustling place. A wagon builder set up shop next door to the general store. Then came a bank and a stable and a barbershop and a newspaper office. The *New Hope Gazette* printed all the news and invitations and signs too. Soon Main Street had shops on both sides and a church with a bell in its steeple at the north end.

"In 1900, Mathilde married Franz's son
Heinrich in that very church, and the whole
town came to celebrate the wedding.
Mathilde and Heinrich moved into a house
on the brand-new street of Maple Lane, and
Heinrich built the New Hope Tannery to
make the best leather gloves and saddles
and boots west of the Appalachian Mountains.

"By 1910, when Mathilde's little boy,
Hans, was four years old, the railroad had
come to New Hope. On it came traveling
actors and salesmen and businessmen and
friends and some people who stayed and
became new citizens."

"And then what, Grandpa?" Jimmy asked.

"And then came me," said Grandpa. "Hans grew up to be my daddy and your great-grandpa."

"Tell about the statue," said Jimmy.

"When I was five years old," said Grandpa, "New Hope built this statue, and your great-grandpa told me the story that I just told you. It's a statue of Lars Jensen—your great-great-great-grandfather—who started this town because his axle broke."

New Hope

by Henri Sorensen

Meet the Author and Illustrator

Henri Sorensen was born in Denmark. As a young boy, he often visited the local art museum once or twice a week. Later he went on to study art at a university in Denmark. He became a freelance illustrator, working mostly for publishing and advertising companies.

The mood of a story is very important to him. He sees the mood of the pictures in his head before he starts to illustrate. He said, *"When I illustrate a book, I always hope that my illustrations will appeal both to grown-ups and to children. I'm often surprised to see how much children notice and how important colors are to them."* "New Hope" is the first book he has both written and illustrated.

Theme Connections

Within the Selection

 Record your answers to the questions below in the Response Journal section of your Writer's Notebook. In small groups, report the ideas you wrote. Discuss your ideas with the rest of the group. Then choose a person to report your group's answers to the class.

- Why did Lars Jensen and his family come to America?

- How did New Hope become a town?

- Why is New Hope a good name for the town started by Lars Jensen?

Across Selections

- How do you think life changed for the first Americans when settlers like Lars Jensen came to America?

Beyond the Selection

- Think about how "New Hope" adds to what you know about our country and its people.

- Add items to the Concept/Question Board about our country and its people.

A Place Called Freedom

Scott Russell Sanders
illustrated by Thomas B. Allen

Down in Tennessee, on the plantation where I was born, Mama worked in the big house and Papa worked in the fields. The master of that big house set us free in the spring of 1832, when I was seven years old and my sister, Lettie, was five.

Papa called Lettie a short drink of water, because she was little and wriggly, and he called me a long gulp of air, because I was tall and full of talk.

As soon as we could pack some food and clothes, we left the plantation, heading north for Indiana. Our aunts and uncles and cousins who were still slaves hugged us hard and waved until we were out of sight.

Papa said it would be safer to travel at night.

"How're we going to find our way in the dark?" I asked him.

"We'll follow the drinking gourd," Papa answered. He pointed to the glittery sky, and I saw he meant the Big Dipper. He showed me how to find the North Star by drawing an arrow from the dipper's lip. Papa loved stars. That's why, when he gave up his old slave's name and chose a new one, he called himself Joshua Starman. And that's why my name is James Starman.

❄

It was a weary, long way. Night after
night as we traveled, the buttery bowl
of the moon filled up, then emptied
again. When Lettie got tired, she rode
on Papa's shoulders for a while, or on
Mama's hip. But I walked the whole
way on my own feet.

At last one morning, just after
sunrise, we came to the Ohio River. A
fisherman with a face as wrinkled as
an old boot carried us over the water in
his boat. On the far shore we set our
feet on the free soil of Indiana. White
flowers covered the hills that day like
feathers on a goose.

By and by we met a Quaker family who took us into their house, gave us seed, and loaned us a mule and a plow, all because they believed that slavery was a sin. We helped on their farm, working shoulder to shoulder, and we planted our own crops.

That first year Papa raised enough corn and wheat for us to buy some land beside the Wabash River, where the dirt was as black as my skin. Papa could grow anything, he could handle horses, and he could build a barn or a bed.

Before winter, Papa and Mama built us a sturdy cabin. Every night we sat by the fire and Papa told stories that made the shadows dance. Every morning Mama held school for Lettie and me. Mama knew how to read and write from helping with lessons for the master's children. She could sew clothes that fit you like the wind, and her cooking made your tongue glad.

While the ground was still frozen, Papa rode south through the cold nights, down to the plantation in Tennessee. We fretted until he showed up again at our door, leading two of my aunts, two uncles, and five cousins. They stayed with us until they could buy land near ours and build their own cabins.

Again and again Papa went back to Tennessee, and each time he came home with more of the folks we loved.

Hearing about our settlement, black people arrived from all over the South, some of them freed like us, some of them runaways. There were carpenters and blacksmiths, basket weavers and barrel makers.

Soon we had a church, then a store, then a stable, then a mill to grind our grain. For the first time in our lives, we had money, just enough to get by, and we watched every penny.

After a few years, the railroad decided to run tracks through our village, because so many people had gathered here. If our place was going to be on the map, it needed a name. At a meeting, folks said we should call it Starman, in honor of Mama and Papa. But Mama and Papa said, "No, let's name it Freedom."

And that's how we came to live in a place called Freedom.

We all celebrated the new name by building a school, where Mama could teach everyone, young and old, to read and write and do sums. She made me want to learn everything there was to know.

When Mama first told me about the alphabet, I wondered how I could ever remember twenty-six different letters. But I learned them all in a flash. It was like magic to me, the way those letters joined up to make words.

Papa's farming was also like magic. He would put seeds in the ground, and before you knew it, here came melon vines or cornstalks. He planted trees, and here came apples or nuts or shade.

For a long while, I couldn't decide whether I wanted to grow up and become a farmer like Papa or a teacher like Mama.

"I don't see why a teacher can't farm," Mama said.

"I don't see why a farmer can't teach," said Papa.

They were right, you know, because I raised the beans and potatoes for supper, and I wrote these words with my own hand.

A Place Called Freedom

Meet the Author

Scott Sanders has written realistic fiction, science fiction, folktales, and stories for children. In his work, he likes to ask questions that scientists might ask. He is concerned about people and how they solve their problems. Many of his writings are about the lives of rural people, children, and the elderly. He said, *"If my writing does not help my neighbors to live more alertly, pleasurably, or wisely, then it is worth little."*

Meet the Illustrator

Thomas B. Allen was born in Tennessee and took his first art class when he was nine years old. His illustrations have appeared in many magazines and over twenty children's books. He tries to combine a feeling of the old and new in his pictures. In addition to painting, he enjoys using a pen-and-ink cross-hatching method.

Theme Connections

Within the Selection

Writer's Notebook Record your answers to the questions below in the Response Journal section of your Writer's Notebook. In small groups, report the ideas you wrote. Discuss your ideas with the rest of the group. Then choose a person to report your group's answers to the class.

- How did the family in this story build a better life for themselves?
- How did the people who joined the family contribute to the new town?
- Why is Freedom a good name for the town in this story?

Across Selections

- How is Freedom like the town of New Hope?

Beyond the Selection

- Think about how "A Place Called Freedom" adds to what you know about our country and its people.
- Add items to the Concept/Question Board about our country and its people.

The Story of the Statue of Liberty

Betsy Maestro
illustrated by Giulio Maestro

The Statue of Liberty stands on an island in New York Harbor. She is a beautiful sight to all who pass by her. Each year, millions of visitors ride the ferry out to the island. They climb to the top of the statue and enjoy the lovely view.

A young French sculptor named Frédéric Auguste Bartholdi visited America in 1871. When he saw Bedloe's Island in New York Harbor, he knew it was just the right place for a statue he wanted to build.

Bartholdi had created many other statues and monuments, but this one was to be very special. It was to be a present from the people of France to the people of America, as a remembrance of the old friendship between the two countries.

When Bartholdi got back to Paris, he made sketches and some small models. The statue would be a woman whom he would call Liberty. She would be a symbol of the freedom in the New World. She would hold a lamp in her raised hand to welcome people who came to America. She would be *Liberty Enlightening the World.*

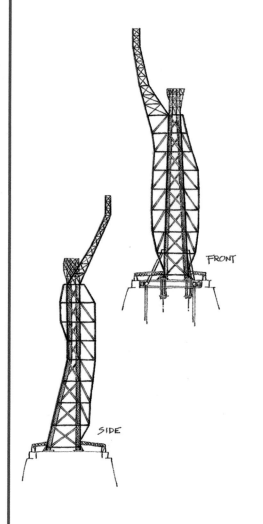

FRONT

SIDE

The statue would be very large and very strong. Bartholdi wanted people to be able to climb up inside the statue and look out over the harbor from the crown and torch.

Many well-known artists, engineers, and craftsmen gave him ideas about how to build the statue. First, a huge skeleton was constructed from strong steel.

Many people worked together in a large workshop. Some worked on Liberty's head and crown. Others worked on her right hand which would hold the torch.

In her left hand she would hold a tablet with the date July 4, 1776, written on it. This is when the Declaration of Independence was signed.

The arm holding the torch was sent to Philadelphia for America's 100th birthday celebration in 1876. Afterward, it stood in Madison Square in New York City for a number of years.

Liberty's head was shown at the World's Fair in Paris during this time. Visitors were able to climb inside and look around. In this way, money was raised to pay for the statue.

Then, skin of gleaming copper was put onto the skeleton and held in place with iron straps. As the huge statue grew, all of Paris watched with great fascination.

Finally, in 1884, Liberty was completed. There was a big celebration in Paris. Many famous people came to see her. Only a few had the energy to climb all the way to the crown— 168 steps!

Then began the hard work of taking Liberty apart for the long voyage across the Atlantic Ocean. Each piece was marked and packed into a crate. There were 214 crates in all. They were carried by train and then put on a ship to America.

But in America people had lost interest in the Statue of Liberty. Money had run out and work on Bedloe's Island had stopped. The base for the statue was not finished. With the help of a large New York newspaper, the money was raised.

People all over the country, including children, sent in whatever they could. By the time the ship reached New York in 1885, it was greeted with new excitement.

The work on the island went on and soon the pedestal was completed. Piece by piece, the skeleton was raised. Then the copper skin was riveted in place. Liberty was put back together like a giant puzzle. The statue had been built not once, but twice!

At last, in 1886, Liberty was standing where she belonged. A wonderful celebration was held. Boats and ships filled the harbor. Speeches were read, songs were sung. Bartholdi himself unveiled Liberty's face and she stood gleaming in all her glory, for everyone to see. There was a great cheer from the crowd. Then President Grover Cleveland gave a speech.

Over the years, immigrants have arrived to begin new lives in America. To them, the Statue of Liberty is a symbol of all their hopes and dreams. She has welcomed millions of people arriving in New York by ship.

Every year, on the Fourth of July, the United States of America celebrates its independence. Fireworks light up the sky above New York Harbor. The Statue of Liberty is a truly unforgettable sight—a symbol of all that is America.

The Story of the Statue of Liberty

Meet the Author

Betsy Maestro was a teacher before she began working with her husband on children's books. She enjoys writing nonfiction books, like "The Story of the Statue of Liberty," for children. She spent months taking notes about the Statue of Liberty in order to write this story. She said, *"Children often become frustrated when a project can't be finished instantly. Our book, we hope, will help them appreciate that it took Bartholdi fifteen years to complete the Statue of Liberty."*

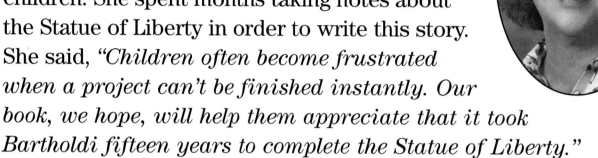

Meet the Illustrator

Giulio Maestro wrote to Walt Kelly, an artist he admired. Mr. Kelly wrote him back, encouraging him to draw every day. *"I think back a lot to the advice Walt Kelly gave me. 'Draw every day. Draw anything and everything you like. The important thing is to draw every day.' It's the same advice I now give children who ask me how they can learn to draw well."*

Mr. Maestro uses a variety of styles and mediums. By using different styles, he can make his work interesting and better describe the mood of the story.

Theme Connections

Within the Selection

Record your answers to the questions below in the Response Journal section of your Writer's Notebook. In small groups, report the ideas you wrote. Discuss your ideas with the rest of the group. Then choose a person to report your group's answers to the class.

- Why did Frederic Auguste Bartholdi want to build the Statue of Liberty?
- Why is the Statue of Liberty such an important landmark?

Across Selections

- Lars Jensen and his family came to America before the Statue of Liberty was completed on the island. Do you think they would have liked Liberty to have welcomed them? Why?

Beyond the Selection

- How did your family come to America? Were any of your relatives welcomed by the Statue of Liberty?
- Think about how "The Story of the Statue of Liberty" adds to what you know about our country and its people.
- Add items to the Concept/Question Board about our country and its people.

Statue of Liberty

Myra Cohn Livingston

Give me your tired, your poor, she says,
Those yearning to be free.
Take a light from my burning torch,
The light of Liberty.

Give me your huddled masses
Lost on another shore,
Tempest-tossed and weary,
These I will take and more.

Give me your thirsty, your hungry
Who come from another place.
You who would dream of freedom
Look into my face.

Focus Questions Why do people want to hold on to their past after moving to a new land? What feelings would you have leaving your home country and the people you love?

The Butterfly Seeds

by Mary Watson

Jake's house was empty, except for the overstuffed trunk in the middle of the floor.

"Sit on it, Mama," Papa instructed.

His sisters giggled as they watched Mama bounce up and down while Papa tried to close the latch.

But Jake just stared out the window. He kept thinking about how much he would miss Grandpa.

When Grandpa came to say good-bye, he brought presents for everyone. But he gave Jake something special.

"They're butterfly seeds," Grandpa said, poking around in the little tin box. "Just plant them in your new garden, and, like magic, you'll have hundreds of butterflies."

"Are you sure they will grow in America, Grandpa?" Jake asked sadly. Grandpa pressed the little box tightly into Jake's hand and nodded.

That evening, Jake's family crowded onto the deck of the great S.S. *Celtic*. Many of the passengers were carrying balls of yarn with the ends trailing over the side of the boat.

When the ship pulled away from the dock, those left behind held the ends and watched the lines stretch out across the ocean. Jake could barely see Grandpa when his yarn-line was pulled from his hand. He reached into his pocket to make sure Grandpa's seeds were safe.

That night, the ship tossed, rolling the passengers back and forth in their narrow bunk beds. Jake couldn't sleep. He reached over and slipped his hand into his jacket pocket.

"What do you have there?" Benny asked. The boys moved closer to the dim cabin light.

"They're butterfly seeds," Jake said, opening the tin.

"What kind of seeds?" a few sleepy-eyed children asked as they crawled down from their bunk.

Then Jake told them about Grandpa's seeds, and the beautiful butterfly garden he would plant in America.

"Look what I'm bringing to America!" Benny exclaimed.

And then the show-and-tell game began. Benny let everyone hold his real gold pocket watch. Jake's sisters paraded their porcelain dolls. There were spinning tops, hand-painted eggs, musical instruments, and even a lucky horseshoe. But everyone agreed that Jake's butterfly seeds were the best of all. Except Albert.

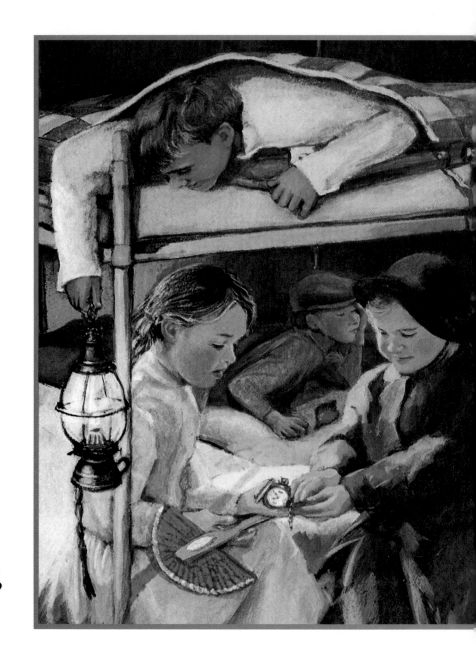

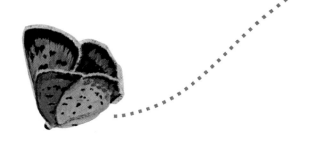

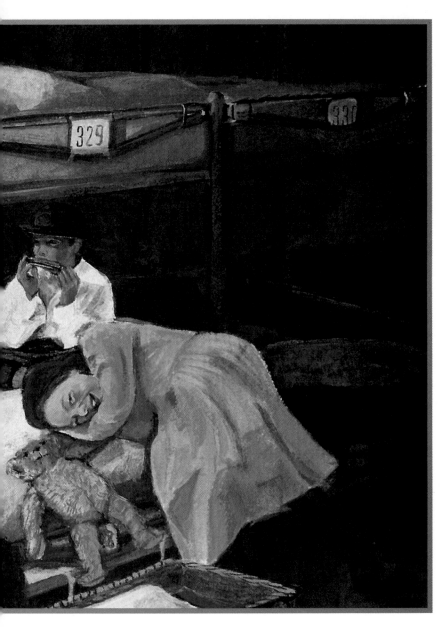

"Whoever heard of butterfly seeds?" he said, and just played his harmonica.

After two long weeks, the ship docked in New York. Papa held tightly to Mama and the children as everyone was herded onto the waiting ferryboats.

When the ferries reached Ellis Island, the passengers were shuffled into long lines to be inspected. Jake's heart raced, as he slowly inched up in line. He wondered if they would take away his seeds. The inspectors looked in Jake's ears and eyes—but not in his pockets. Grandpa's seeds were safe!

Finally, Jake and his family arrived at their new home on Market Street. Papa led the family up three flights of stairs to two small rooms.

Jake looked out at the dark narrow alley, cluttered with lines of drying clothes. *Where can I plant Grandpa's seeds?* he worried.

The next morning, Jake was up early. Below, he spotted a fruit vendor emptying a crate of apples into his cart.

"Could I have that empty crate, sir?" he yelled down.

Before Mr. Gargiulo could figure out where the question had come from, Jake was standing breathlessly beside him.

"I'm going to make a window box . . . so I can plant my grandpa's seeds in it . . . and that's why I need the crate," he blurted out.

"You can have the crate, boy, but I don't think it's any good for planting seeds." Mr. Gargiulo wiggled his fingers between the slats.

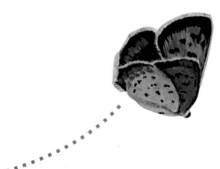

"All you need is a piece of burlap to fix that," called Mr. Lingchow, the fish peddler.

He emptied his catch into an icy bin and handed Jake the empty bag. Jake opened the seam with his pocketknife and spread the burlap evenly inside the crate.

Jake hurried across the street to the blacksmith shop to show Papa. It was Papa's first day at his new job, and he didn't pay much attention when Jake asked for his advice.

"I need a way to keep this crate from falling off our windowsill," Jake shouted over the ring of the anvil.

"Maybe I can help you," someone hollered. It was Mr. O'Malley, the shop owner. He knew just what Jake needed. He hammered two bars of red-hot metal into a strong pair of window-box hangers.

After work, Papa nailed the box into place. Jake rigged up a clothesline and a pulley to hoist up buckets of dirt from the alley. All of the neighborhood children wanted to help. All except for Albert, who played his harmonica instead.

It was a hot summer. Jake and his new friends climbed the fire escape every day to check the window box. They would hang over the railing and search through the bushy plants for butterflies.

"Maybe your silly old grandpa got the seeds mixed up," Albert would mutter.

Jake began to wonder if Grandpa's seeds were magic or just a story made up for a homesick boy.

Then one day the sky rumbled, and a sudden shower drenched the hot, steaming streets.

When the sun reappeared, merchants and shoppers filled the street once more. The children went back to their play.

Suddenly, Mr. Gargiulo called out, "Look at that beautiful butterfly."

The children chased the butterfly through the crowded street until it flew up to Jake's window box.

"Look at them all!" Albert shouted.

Jake heard Albert's yell and opened his window.

"They're finally here, Grandpa!" Jake whispered, as if Grandpa were listening. "Your butterflies are here . . . and they like America too."

The Butterfly Seeds

Meet the Author and Illustrator

Mary Watson's husband wrote the first picture book she illustrated. Her grandfather inspired her second book, "The Butterfly Seeds." Her grandparents met on the boat on their trip to the United States. Her grandfather brought seeds from England, and her grandmother brought seeds from Ireland. He told her many stories of the trip.

Ms. Watson finds painting people and faces more interesting than painting a landscape. She and her family live in New Jersey. They operate a historical farm. She often illustrates and writes materials for the farm.

Theme Connections

Within the Selection

Writer's Notebook Record your answers to the questions below in the Response Journal section of your Writer's Notebook. In small groups, report the ideas you wrote. Discuss your ideas with the rest of the group. Then choose a person to report your group's answers to the class.

- How did the butterfly seeds help Jake adjust to his new home in America?
- Why do you think Jake received so much help from people in the neighborhood?

Across Selections

- What did Jake's family have in common with the Jensen family in "New Hope"?
- What might Jake have seen as his ship arrived in New York?

Beyond the Selection

- Think about how "The Butterfly Seeds" adds to what you know about our country and its people.
- Add items to the Concept/Question Board about our country and its people.

The Oregon Trail. 1869. **Albert Bierstadt.** Oil on canvas.
The Butler Institute of American Art, Youngstown, Ohio.

***The Telegram,
Detention Room,
Ellis Island.*** 1922.
Martha Walter. Oil on
canvas. 14 × 18 in. The
National Museum of
Women in the Arts,
Washington, D.C.

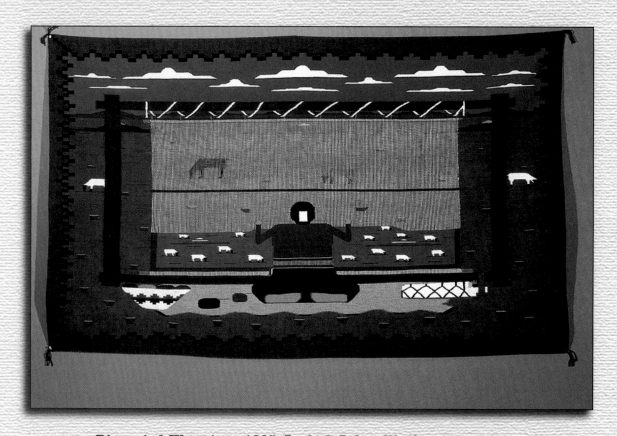

Pictorial Weaving. 1885. **Isabel John.** Wool, commercial,
and natural dyes. 48 × 77 $\frac{1}{2}$ in. Collection of The Birmingham
Museum of Art, Birmingham, Alabama.

Focus Questions Are there still immigrants coming to
America today? How would you feel if you had to leave your
country and all your possessions?

A Piece of Home

by Sonia Levitin
illustrated by Juan Wijngaard

Gregor and his family are moving to America.
They have waited for a long, long time.

"When we go to America," says Gregor's mother,
"you will see your cousin Elie. He is the same
age as you."

Ever since Gregor was a baby, he has heard
about Cousin Elie. On Mama's bureau is a picture
of Cousin Elie with Aunt Marissa and Uncle Ivan.
They are standing in front of a small wooden
house in America. Around the house are some
trees and a fence.

Gregor has never seen a house like this. He lives in an apartment building with many floors and an elevator and the sounds of other families singing through the halls. Cousin Elies's house in America looks strange. Gregor is not sure he wants to go there.

But the time has come. They must pack. Gregor
has a suitcase of his own.

"We cannot take much," says Mama.

"Only one special treasure for each of us," says Papa.
"Something to share with our family in America."

Baby Katje takes her teething ring made of elk
horn. This she will not share.

Papa says, "I must take my garmoshka, for how could I live in America without music?"

Mama says, "I will take our small samovar. My sister Marissa always loved our good Russian Tea." Whenever Mama talks about her sister Marissa, she looks as if she will start to cry.

Gregor does not know what to take to America. The beautiful painted chair his father's friend made for him? The ice skates that are still almost new? The brass harness bells he loves to hear on a winter's night?

Gregor does not want to leave anything behind. But Mama and Papa say he must choose. It is too expensive to bring everything to America. Besides, in a new land people like new things.

The last night arrives. Still Gregor cannot decide what to take. Papa is cross. Mama wrings her hands. Even Baby Katje is fussy.

When Gregor is cold or tired or unhappy, he knows what to do. He runs and gets the blanket Great-grandmother made. It is warm and soft and pretty.

Gregor gathers up the blanket. "I will take this to America," he says.

Mama looks tired. "It is too big to pack," she says.

"I will carry it," says Gregor.

"It will get dirty," Mama says.

Papa says, "Look, if you come with a blanket, your cousin Elie will think you are a baby."

Gregor says, "I want my blanket."

Mama sighs and looks at Papa.

Papa nods and says, "Very well. At least it is settled."

The long journey begins at the airport, filled
with noise. The plane starts with a loud roar.
Baby Katje screams, and Mama tries to rock her
to sleep.

Gregor sits between Mama and Papa, holding
tight to the seat belt around his middle. The sky
turns dark. Gregor is almost asleep, but they
have to leave this plane and wait for another
plane to take them to America.

Gregor is so tired. He wishes he were home. He
lies down on a chair, wrapped in his blanket.

At last they get onto another plane. It is cold. Gregor puts his blanket over his head and sleeps.

The smell of food wakes him. Supper comes on little white plastic trays. Gregor likes the potatoes and the round white roll and the golden peaches. The other food tastes strange.

"Eat your meat," says Mama. "Eat your beans."

Gregor shakes his head. "I'm not hungry," he says. "I want to go home." He feels tears in his eyes.

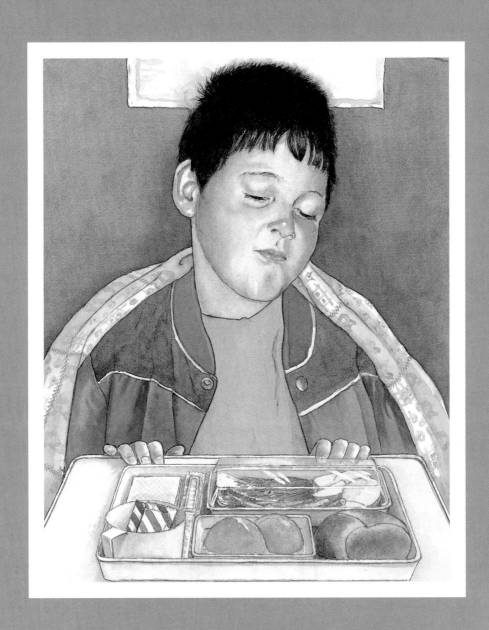

A nice lady brings him small toys. There is a tiny
airplane, crayons, a coloring book. But Gregor
does not feel like playing. He is thinking of his
friends at home, and of his teacher at day school.
Now Gregor is sure he does not want to go to
America. But he tells the lady "thank you," new
words he has learned. His cousin Elie speaks
perfect English. He also speaks Russian. Everyone
says how smart Elie is in school.

Why do they have to go to America? Gregor has asked his parents many times.

"In America," Papa says proudly, "work is waiting for me." Papa works with wood, making beautiful cabinets.

"In America," Mama says happily, "we will not be lonely. We will be with our family."

Now Gregor pulls his blanket tight around himself. Finally he sleeps again.

❧❧❧

"Wake up!" Papa says. "We're almost there."

Light comes into the plane. People stretch and find their things.

Baby Katje is fast asleep.

Gregor feels a flutter in his stomach. Will he like Cousin Elie? Gregor looks down at the blanket. There is a hole in it. The colors are faded. Gregor wishes he had listened to Papa and left the blanket at home. But it is too late.

Mama folds the blanket into a small bundle and puts it in Gregor's lap.

Now Gregor is sure that Cousin Elie will laugh at him and call him a baby. Maybe he should just leave the blanket here on the airplane. Gregor cannot decide.

With a rush of sound, a swoop of motion, the plane lands. Papa leads the family out of the plane.

"Are we here?" asks Gregor. "Where is Cousin Elie?"

But nobody answers him. Papa and Mama are busy with passports and papers. They wait in line so long that Gregor's foot goes to sleep. At last they move out to a large room.

A man and a woman rush over. The man catches Gregor and holds him up high. The woman covers Gregor's face with kisses. The woman smiles, then weeps, then laughs. She looks a little like Mama.

"Welcome! Welcome to America!" say Aunt Marissa and Uncle Ivan.

Katje squeals and claps her hands. Everyone laughs.

Now Gregor sees the little boy standing behind
Aunt Marissa.

"What's the matter with you, Elie?" says Aunt Marissa.
"Come out and say hello!"

Mama gives Gregor a little push and tells him,
"Gregor, this is your cousin Elie. Say hello!"

Cousin Elie says hello in the small voice of a mouse.
He is wearing boots and a leather vest with fringes,
just like a cowboy. Gregor tries to hide his blanket
behind his back; it is too big.

The men talk and laugh. The women hug and kiss, then Aunt Marissa takes Baby Katje in her arms. Gregor does not like the way Cousin Elie is looking at him.

"Why are we standing here?" shouts Uncle Ivan. "Come on! Let's go!"

Everyone squeezes into Uncle Ivan's car, with suitcases on top and in between. Gregor sits on Papa's lap, still holding his blanket. Cousin Elie sits in front with his parents.

Soon they stop at a house. It is so big! "Five rooms," says Uncle Ivan, laughing and nodding. "Five rooms! Well, well, that's how it is in America. Soon you will have a house of your own. In the meantime you will stay with us."

First they eat. There is plenty. Gregor feels empty inside, but he eats only one olive and a cracker.

Cousin Elie eats and stares at Gregor.

Uncle Ivan brings in the coffee.

Aunt Marissa says, "Ah, I remember the good Russian tea we used to make from the samovar at home."

Mama jumps up. When she comes back, she is holding the small samovar, smiling like a queen.

Aunt Marissa fills it with water for tea.

Uncle Ivan pats his full belly and says, "There is nothing like a song after a meal."

Papa hurries out. In a moment he is back holding his garmoshka, already playing and singing.

The grown-ups all sing.

At home Gregor would sing too. But Cousin Elie is staring at him, making faces. Now Gregor wishes he had never come to America. Gregor pulls his blanket close to his chest. He wants to hide inside it and never come out.

The song ends. Suddenly Cousin Elie points at Gregor and shouts, "That's my blanket!"

"No," cry all the parents. "Of course not. How could it be?"

Aunt Marissa comes close to Gregor. She bends down to look at the blanket. Softly she asks Mama, "Is this the blanket Great-grandmother made?"

"Yes," says Mama. "Great-grandmother gave it to our mother on her wedding day."

Aunt Marissa is laughing now. "I remember when I was a little girl. Mama wrapped me up in that blanket."

Papa says, "When Gregor was born, we carried him home in that blanket."

"At one time," Mama says, "the blanket was twice as big. I don't know what happened to the rest."

Aunt Marissa and Cousin Elie whisper together. "Wait!" says Aunt Marissa. She and Cousin Elie run upstairs.

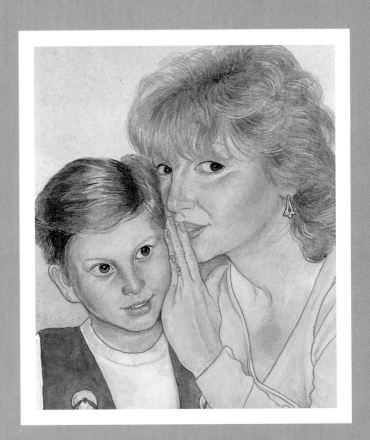

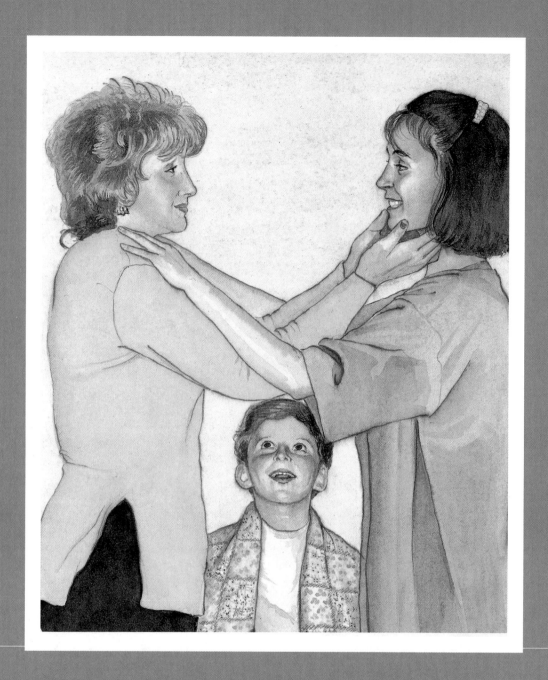

When they return, Cousin Elie has a funny look on his face. He is wearing a blanket exactly like Gregor's.

Aunt Marissa says, "We cut the blanket in half, so I could bring a piece of home with me to America. Don't you remember?"

Now Mama is drying her eyes. "I don't remember a thing," she says, "except how much I missed you."

Elie takes Gregor by the arm. "Want to go out and play?" he asks.

"Okay," says Gregor. It was the first English word he ever learned. "Okay!" says Gregor once again. He likes the sound of this word. It is very American. It makes him smile.

A Piece of Home

Meet the Author

Sonia Levitin was born in Berlin, Germany in 1934. Since childhood, Sonia Levitin has loved books. When she was eleven years old she knew she wanted to become a writer. Many of her books are about things that happened when she was growing up.

Meet the Illustrator

Juan Wijngaard was born in Argentina, and loved drawing from a very young age. His mother was a painter. When he grew up, he too wanted to be a painter. However, when he was asked to illustrate a children's book, he decided to be an illustrator instead. Since then, he has illustrated over twenty books and has been awarded many awards for his illustrations.

Theme Connections

Within the Selection

Record your answers to the questions below in the Response Journal section of your Writer's Notebook. In small groups, report the ideas you wrote. Discuss your ideas with the rest of the group. Then choose a person to report your group's answers to the class.

- Why do you think Gregor was nervous about moving to America?
- How did the blanket help Gregor make friends with his cousin in America?

Across Selections

- Compare how Gregor in this story and Jake in "The Butterfly Seeds" were able to adjust to life in America.
- Spider in "Brave as a Mountain Lion" needed courage to be in the spelling bee. Do you think Gregor needed courage to come to America? Why?

Beyond the Selection

- If you could only choose one item to bring to another country, what would it be? Why?
- Think about how "A Piece of Home" adds to what you know about our country and its people.
- Add items to the Concept/Question Board about our country and its people.

Jalapeño Bagels

Natasha Wing
illustrated by Robert Casilla

"**W**hat should I bring to school on Monday for International Day?" I ask my mother. "My teacher told us to bring something from our culture."

"You can bring a treat from the *panaderia*," she suggests. Panaderia is what Mama calls our bakery. "Help us bake on Sunday—then you can pick out whatever you want."

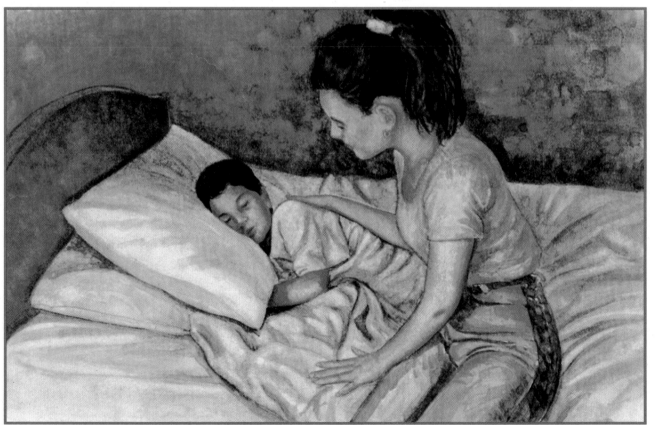

"It's a deal," I tell her. I like helping at the bakery. It's warm there, and everything smells so good.

Early Sunday morning, when it is still dark, my mother wakes me up.

"Pablo, it's time to go to work," she says.

We walk down the street to the bakery. My father turns on the lights. My mother turns on the ovens. She gets out the pans and ingredients for *pan dulce*. Pan dulce is Mexican sweet bread.

I help my mother mix and knead the dough. She shapes rolls and loaves of bread and slides them into the oven. People tell her she makes the best pan dulce in town.

"Maybe I'll bring pan dulce to school," I tell her.

Next we make *empanadas de calabaza*—
pumpkin turnovers. I'm in charge of
spooning the pumpkin filling. Mama folds
the dough in half and presses the edges with
a fork. She bakes them until they are flaky
and golden brown. Some customers come to
our bakery just for her turnovers.

"Maybe I'll bring empanadas de calabaza
instead."

"You'll figure it out," she says. "Ready to make *chango* bars?" Chango means "monkey man."

Mama lets me pour in the chocolate chips and nuts. When she's not looking, I pour in more chocolate chips.

"I could bring chango bars. They're my favorite dessert."

"Mine, too," says Mama. "This batch should be especially good. I put in extra chips."

My father calls from the back room.
"Pablo! Come help me with the bagels!"
Papa speaks English and Yiddish. He learned
Yiddish from his family in New York City.
I know some words, too. *Bubbe* means
"grandmother." He uses my bubbe's recipe
to make the bagels.

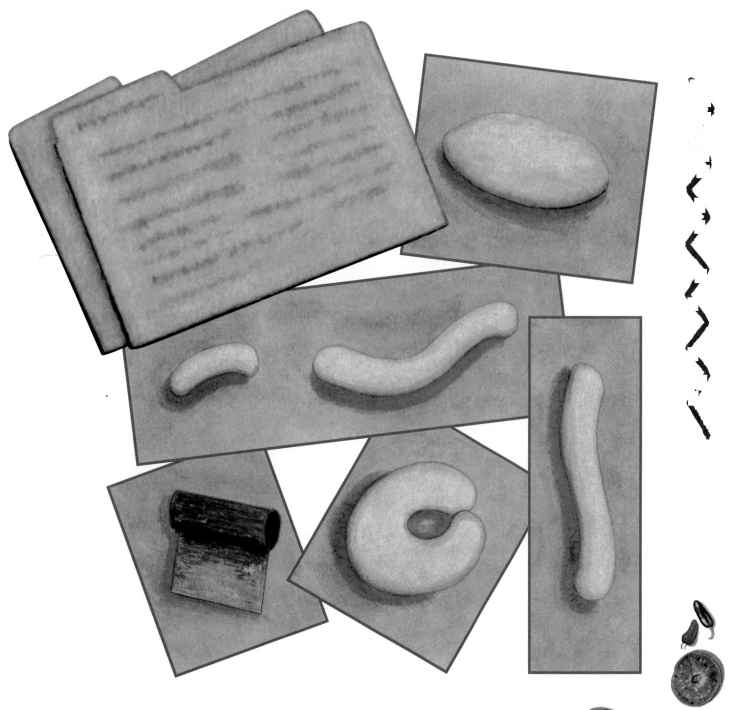

First he makes the dough in a big metal bowl. Then he rolls it out into a long rope shape. He cuts off pieces and shows me how to connect the ends in a circle. We put the circles on trays where they sit and rise.

While we are waiting my father makes *challah*, Jewish braided bread. He lets me practice braiding challah dough at my own counter. It's a lot like braiding hair. The customers say it is almost too beautiful to eat.

"Maybe I'll bring a loaf of challah to school," I tell Papa. He smiles.

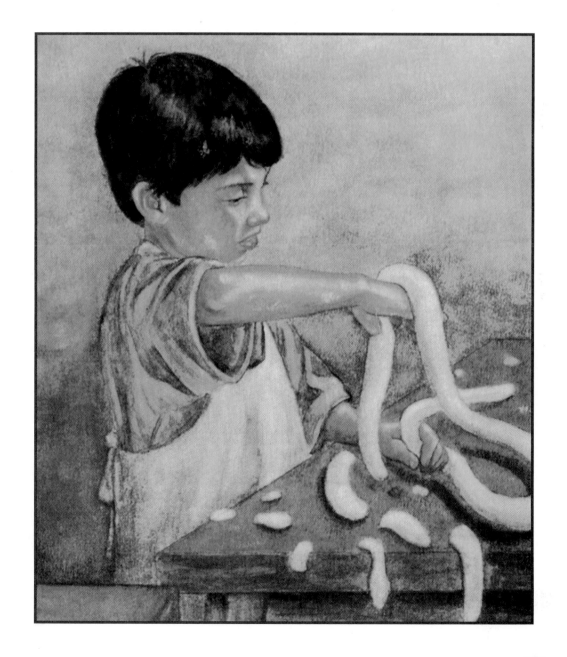

When the bagel dough has risen, he boils the bagels in a huge pot of water and fishes them out with a long slotted spoon. I sprinkle on poppy seeds and sesame seeds, and then they go in the oven.

"Maybe I could bring sesame-seed bagels with cream cheese."

"No *lox?*" Lox is smoked salmon. My father's favorite bagel is pumpernickel with a smear of cream cheese and lox.

I crinkle my nose. "Lox tastes like fish. Jam is better."

My mother joins us and helps my father make another batch of bagels—*jalapeño* bagels. My parents use their own special recipe. While Papa kneads the dough, Mama chops the jalapeño *chiles*. She tosses them into the dough and adds dried red peppers. We roll, cut, make circles, and let them rise. I can't wait until they are done because I am getting hungry.

"Have you decided what you're going to bring to school?" asks Mama.

"It's hard to choose. Everything is so good," I tell her. I look at Papa. "Except for lox."

"You should decide before we open," warns Mama, "or else our customers will buy everything up."

I walk past all the sweet breads, chango bars, and bagels.

I think about my mother and my father and all the different things they make in the bakery.

And suddenly I know exactly what I'm going to bring.

"Jalapeño bagels," I tell my parents. "And I'll spread them with cream cheese and jam."

"Why jalapeño bagels?" asks Papa.

"Because they are a mixture of both of you. Just like me!"

Jalapeño Bagels

Meet the Author

Natasha Wing was born in Milford, Connecticut. Her first job was working at a newspaper. She later worked for an advertising agency. She is now the owner of a writing company.

She became interested in writing children's books after reading one as an adult. She said, *"When you put two things together, such as a story and illustrations, the result is greater than what you expected."* "Jalapeño Bagels" is her second book for children.

Meet the Illustrator

Robert Casilla was born in Jersey City, New Jersey. He began illustrating after graduating from the School of Visual Arts. He said, *"I find great rewards and satisfaction in illustrating for children."* He enjoys working with watercolors for his illustrations. Many of his illustrations are for biographies. When he illustrates a biography, he tries to learn a lot about the person. Knowing the person very well helps him when he works on the art.

Theme Connections

Within the Selection

Writer's Notebook

Record your answers to the questions below in the Response Journal section of your Writer's Notebook. In small groups, report the ideas you wrote. Discuss your ideas with the rest of the group. Then choose a person to report your group's answers to the class.

- Why does Pablo have a hard time choosing what to bring to school on International Day?
- Why did he decide to bring jalapeño bagels?

Across Selections

- What might Gregor from "A Piece of Home" have brought to share for International Day?

Beyond the Selection

- What could you share with others that would tell about your culture?
- Think about how "Jalapeño Bagels" adds to what you know about our country and its people.
- Add items to the Concept/Question Board about our country and its people.

Pronunciation Key

a as in **a**t

ā as in l**a**te

â as in c**a**re

ä as in f**a**ther

e as in s**e**t

ē as in m**e**

i as in **i**t

ī as in k**i**te

o as in **o**x

ō as in r**o**se

ô as in b**ou**ght and r**aw**

oi as in c**oi**n

o͝o as in b**oo**k

o͞o as in t**oo**

or as in f**or**m

ou as in **ou**t

u as in **u**p

ū as in **u**se

ûr as in t**ur**n, g**er**m, l**ear**n, f**ir**m, w**or**k

ə as in **a**bout, chick**e**n, penc**i**l, cann**o**n, circ**u**s

ch as in **ch**air

hw as in **wh**ich

ng as in ri**ng**

sh as in **sh**op

th as in **th**in

t͡h as in **th**ere

zh as in trea**s**ure

The mark (´) is placed after a syllable with a heavy accent, as in **chicken** (chik´ ən).

The mark (´) after a syllable shows a lighter accent, as in **disappear** (dis´ ə pēr´).

Glossary

A

acrobatic (ak′ rə bat′ ik) *adv.* Moving in a skilled and difficult way.

admire (əd mīr′) *v.* To look at or speak of with great appreciation and pleasure.

advice (əd vīs′) *n.* Someone's opinion of what another should do.

allergic (ə lûr′ jik) *adj.* Having an annoying or dangerous reaction to something.

alley (al′ ē) *n.* A narrow street or passageway between or behind buildings.

amber (am′ bər) *n.* A glass-like fossil made from the sap of very old trees.

analyze (an′ ə līz) *v.* To examine very closely.

ancient (ān′ shənt) *adj.* From long ago.

antelope (an′ təl ōp′) *n.* An animal similar to a deer.

anvil (an′ vəl) *n.* A heavy metal block on which hot metal is hammered and shaped.

ashamed (ə shāmd′) *adj.* Feeling shame; upset or guilty because one has done something wrong or silly.

avalanche (av′ ə lanch′) *n.* A large amount of snow, ice, or stones falling rapidly down the side of a mountain.

axle (ak′ səl) *n.* A rod on which the wheels of a wagon turn.

B

bead (bēd) *v.* To make something by stringing beads together.

beam (bēm) *n.* A ray of light.

big house (big hous) *n.* The house on a plantation in which the owner of the plantation lives.

blacksmith (blak′ smith′) *n.* A person who makes things out of iron.

C

blubber (blub´ ûr) *n.* A layer of fat under the skin of whales, seals, and other sea animals. The oil made from whale blubber used to be burned in lamps.

brisk (brisk) *adj.* Quick and lively.

buffalo (buf´ ə lō´) *n.* A large North American animal that has a big shaggy head with short horns and a hump on its back; bison.

buoy (boo´ ē) *v.* To cause to float.

bureau (byûr´ ō) *n.* A dresser for storing clothes.

burrow (bûr´ ō) *v.* To dig a tunnel in the earth.

bustling (bus´ ling) *adj.* Filled with activity.

by and by (bī ənd bī) *adv.* Soon.

canteen (kan tēn´) *n.* A small container for water.

celebrate (sel´ ə brāt´) *v.* To observe or honor a special day or event with ceremonies and other activities.

character (kar´ ik tər) *n.* A person's honesty and honor.

charm (chärm) *n.* An object worn to bring good luck.

citizen (sit´ i zən) *n.* A person who was born in a country or who chooses to live in and become a member of a country.

clearing (klēr´ ing) *v.* To remove or remove things from.

climate (klī´ mit) *n.* The weather in an area.

clue (kloo) *n.* A hint to help figure something out.

coal (kōl) *n.* A black mineral from the earth that can be burned for fuel.

colossal (kə los´ əl) *adj.* Huge; very, very big.

conifer (kon´ ə fûr) *n.* Tree that has cones such as pine or fir.

counterpane (koun´ tər pān´) *n.* A bed covering.

courage (kûr´ ij) *n.* The strength to overcome fear and face danger; bravery.

cradle board (krā´ dəl bord) *n.* A board on which an infant is tied and carried on someone's back.

creepy (krē´ pē) *adj.* Makes you feel like something is crawling over your skin.

crinkle (kring´ kəl) *v.* To scrunch up; wrinkle.

D

dangle (dang´ gəl) *v.* To hang loosely.

demand (di mand´) *v.* To say that something should belong to one; to claim as one's own.

depend (di pend´) *v.* To trust; to count on someone for help.

difficult (dif´ i kult) *adj.* Needing much effort; not easy.

dike (dīk) *n.* A thick wall built to hold back water.

dinosaur (dīn´ ə sôr) *n.* Any of the large group of extinct, prehistoric animals that lived long ago.

disappear (dis´ ə pēr´) *v.* 1. To leave someone's sight; to stop being seen. 2. To stop living.

discovery (dis kəv´ ə rē) *n.* The act of seeing or finding out something for the first time.

doctorate (dok´ tər it) *n.* An award for graduating from the highest level of college; a doctoral degree.

doe (dō) *n.* A female deer.

dough (dō) *n.* A thick mixture of flour, liquid, and other ingredients that is usually baked. Dough is used to make bread, cookies, pie crusts, and other food.

dread (dred) *v.* To feel fearful or unhappy about something.

drench (drench´) *v.* To soak with water.

drift (drift) *v.* To pile up in masses from the action of the wind.

drinking gourd (dring´ king gord) *n.* The hard-shelled fruit of a vining plant that is hollowed out and used to dip water.

drinking gourd

E

earthquake (ûrth´ kwāk´) *n.* An underground shock that makes part of the Earth's surface shake.

echo (ek´ ō) *n.* A sound that seems to be repeated because it is thrown back from far away.

elevator (el´ ə vā´ tûr) *n.* A device in a building that moves people or things up and down.

elk (elk) *n.* A large member of the deer family.

embed (em bed´) *v.* To set something into a material.

emblem (em´ bləm) *n.* Sign; symbol.

enormous (i nôr´ məs) *adj.* Huge; very big.

erupt (i rupt´) *v.* To burst out; to explode.

exclaim (iks klām´) *v.* To cry out suddenly.

expert (eks´ pûrt) *n.* A person who knows a lot about something.

extinct (eks tingkt´) *adj.* No longer alive.

F

fair (fâr) *adj.* Not in favor of any one more than another or others; just.

fascination (fa´ sē nā´ shēn) *n.* A strong attraction.

ferry (fâr´ ē) *n.* A medium-size boat or raft. —*v.* To carry something over water by boat.

fetch (fech) *v.* To go after and bring back; get.

flood (flud) *v.* To cover with water.

ford (ford) *v.* To cross directly through the water of a river.

forge (forj) *n.* A workshop that makes objects out of metal heated in a large furnace.

formula (for´ myə lə) *n.* Steps used to come up with an amount.

fossil (fos´ əl) *n.* The hardened remains or traces of an animal or plant that lived long ago.

fret (fret) *v.* To worry.

fringe (frinj´) *n.* A border on clothes made of hanging threads.

G

garmoshka (gar mōsh´ kə) *n.* A small accordion used in Russia.

gather (gath´ ər) *v.* Collects by folding together.

gleaming (glēm´ ing) *adj.* Shining brightly.

gurgling (gûr´ gling) *adj.* Making a noise like bubbling water.

gushing (gush´ ing) *v.* To pour out suddenly and in large amounts.

guts (guts) *n. slang.* Courage; bravery.

gymnasium (jim nā´ zē əm) *n.* A room or building with equipment for physical exercise or training and for indoor sports.

H

harbor (har´ bər) *n.* A sheltered place along a coast. Ships and boats often anchor in a harbor.

hardened (hard´ ən) *v.* Became firm.

harmonica (har´ mon i kə) *n.* A musical instrument. It is a small case with slots that contain a series of metal reeds. It is played by blowing in and out through the slots.

harness (har´ nis) *n.* Leather straps used to fasten a horse to a plow, wagon, or carriage.

hatch (hach) *v.* To cause young to come from an egg.

hero (hēr´ō) *n.* A person who does brave or important things to help others.

homesick (hōm´sik´) *adj.* Sad due to wanting to go home; missing one's home.

huddled (hu´dəld) *adj.* Gathered together closely.

I

Iguanodon (i gwä´nə don´) *n.* A dinosaur that walked on two feet and ate only plants.

imprint (im´print) *n.* An image left when an object is pressed into something.

independence (in´də pen´dəns) *n.* Not being under the control of others; freedom.

ingredient (in grē´dē ənt) *n.* Any one of the parts that go into a mixture.

inspector (in spek´tər) *n.* A person who makes inspections.

instruction (in struk´shən) *n.* The act of teaching.

international (in´tər nash´ə nəl) *adj.* Having to do with two or more nations.

invitation (in və tā´shən) *n.* A written or spoken request to do something.

issue (ish´ōō) *v.* To publish; to send out.

J

jalapeño (ho´lə pā´nyō) *n.* A Mexican hot pepper.

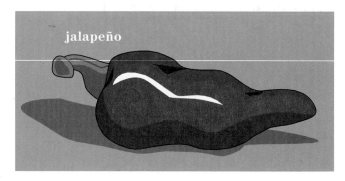
jalapeño

journey (jûr´nē) *n.* A trip from one place to another.

K

knead (nēd) *v.* To form into a ball and press over and over with the hands.

L

lack (lak) *n.* A need; a shortage; not enough of something.

lagoon (lə go͞on´) *n.* A small body of water connected to a larger lake, river, or sea.

limestone (līm´ stōn´) *n.* A type of rock used for building.

livestock (līv´ stok) *n.* Farm animals, such as cows, sheep, horses, or pigs. —*adj.* Having to do with such animals.

lodge (loj) *n.* A small house, cottage, or cabin.

M

mammoth (mam´ əth) *n.* A large elephant-like animal that lived long ago.

mass (mas) *n.* A large group of people.

medicine man (med´ i sin man´) *n.* A person in certain North American Indian tribes who was called upon to cure sickness and was believed to have magic powers.

mineral (min´ ər əl) *n.* Something found underground, like gold or coal.

minister (min´ ə stər) *n.* 1. A person who helps a king or queen rule. 2. A pastor; the leader in a church.

mixture (miks´ chər) *n.* Something made up of different things together.

moisture (mois´ chər) *n.* Water or other liquid in the air or on a surface; slight wetness.

mold (mōld) *n.* A hollow form made in a special shape. A liquid or soft material is poured into a mold. When it hardens, it takes the shape of the mold.

monument (mon´ yə mənt) *n.* A structure built to honor someone or something important.

mound (mound) *n.* A hill or heap of earth, stones, or other material.

mural (myûr´ əl) *n.* A large painting, often on a wall.

mutter (mu´ tər) *v.* To say something angrily loud enough for only the speaker to hear.

mysterious (mis tēr´ ē əs) *adj.* Making others curious or surprised; causing others to wonder.

N

neighborhood (nā´ bər hood´) *n.* A person who lives in a house or apartment next to or near one's own.

numb (num) *adj.* Having no feeling; not able to feel anything in some part of the body.

O

ooze (ōōz) *n.* Slush; slime; watery mud.

opinion (ə pin´ yən) *n.* Belief about a given topic.

overstuffed (ō´ vər stuft´) *adj.* Having more in it than it can easily hold.

P

paleontologist (pā´ lē ən tol´ ə jist) *n.* Scientists who study life from long ago.

passenger (pas´ ən jûr) *n.* A person who travels in a vehicle.

passport (pas´ port) *n.* A paper that allows a person to go from one country to another.

peat (pēt) *n.* Matter covering the ground in a forest and made up of partly decayed plants and moss.

pedestal (pe´ dəs təl) *n.* A base that something sits on.

peg (peg) *n.* A piece of wood used to hang things on.

pinky (ping´ kē) *n.* The little finger on a person's hand; the finger farthest from the thumb.

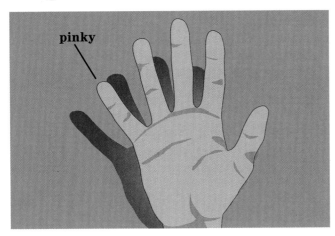

pinky

pith helmet (pith hel´ mit) *n.* A lightweight hat that shields a person's head from the sun.

plains (plāns) *n.* An area of flat or almost flat land.

plantation (plan tā´ shən) *n.* A very large farm where crops like rice, cotton, or sugar are grown.

platter (pla´ tər) *n.* A large plate.

potlatches (pot´ lach əs) *n.* A gift-giving party held by certain North American Indian tribes.

powerful (pou ûr fəl) *adj.* Having great power.

prehistoric (prē´ hi stor´ ik) *adj.* Belonging to a time many years ago, before history was written down.

prejudice (prej´ ə dis) *n.* Unfairness; an opinion formed without knowing the facts.

preserve (pri zûrv´) *v.* To protect from spoiling.

proclamation (prok´ lə mā´ shən) *n.* A public announcement; a statement to the people.

prodigious (prə dij´ əs) *adj.* Enormous; monstrous.

protection (prō´ tek shən) *n.* The keeping of someone or something from harm.

protest (prō´ test) *n.* A public demonstration of objection.

puff (puf) *n.* A short, gentle burst of air, breath, smoke, or something similar.

Q

qualify (kwô´ lə fī´) *v.* To have the knowledge needed to do a certain task.

R

recipe (res´ i pē´) *n.* A list of ingredients and instructions for making something to eat or drink.

recycling (rē sī´ kling) *v.* To make fit to be used again.

remembrance (ri mem´ brəns) *n.* An object meant to remind one of something good.

reply (ri plī´) *v.* To answer.

rescue (res´ kū) *v.* To save or free.

reservation (re´ zər vā´ shən) *n.* A piece of public land set aside for Native Americans.

reverse (ri vûrs´) *n.* The opposite way; backward.

riot (rī ət) *n.* A noisy and violent disorder caused by a crowd of people.

rot (rot) *v.* Decay until nothing is left.

rumble (rum´ bəl) *v.* To make a low, rolling sound like thunder.

Russian (rush´ ən) *adj.* From Russia.

S

samovar (sam´ ə var) *n.* A kettle used to heat water for tea.

scientist (sī´ ən tist) *n.* A person who studies nature and natural laws.

scroll (skrōl) *n.* A roll of paper used for writing, especially many years ago.

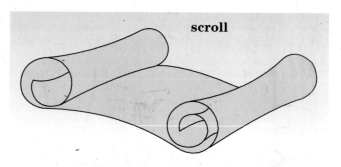

scroll

sediment (sed´ ə mənt) *n.* Matter that sinks to the bottom of water.

seek (sēk) *v.* To look for; to try to find.

seep (sēp) *v.* To leak into.

Seismosaurus (sīs′ mə sor′ əs) *n.* A dinosaur that was about 110 feet long and 50 feet tall.

settlement (set′ əl mənt) *n.* A small village or group of houses.

shallow (shal′ ō) *adj.* Being close to the bottom.

shoo (sho͞o) *v.* To drive or send away.

Shoshone (shə shō′ nē) *n.* A Native American group originally from the western United States. —*adj.* Having to do with this group.

shove (shuv) *v.* To push with force.

shuffle (shu′ fəl) *v.* To mix together in a confused way.

slat (slat) *n.* A flat strip of wood.

sluggish (slug′ ish) *adj.* Moving slowly.

soot (so͝ot) *n.* Tiny, black bits of something that has burned, such as wood or coal.

sought (sôt) *v.* Looked for; tried to find

spirit (spēr′ ət) *n.* An unseen being or force that guides and watches out for another.

sprinkler (spring′ klər) *n.* A device that scatters drops of water.

stable (stā′ bəl) *n.* A building in which tame animals, especially horses, are kept.

starve (starv) *v.* To suffer from or die of hunger.

strange (strānj) *adj.* Odd or not familiar.

stupendous (stə pen′ dəs) *adj.* Amazingly large.

sturdy (stûr′ dē) *adj.* Well built; very strong; not easily broken.

succeed (sək sēd′) *v.* To take someone's job after that person quits; to follow in a job after someone else.

successor (sək ses′ ər) *n.* A person who takes over another person's job.

swamp (swomp) *n.* An area of low, wet ground; a marsh.

swampy (swom′ pē) *adj.* A wet and muddy area.

swarm (sworm) *n.* A large group of people or animals.

swat (swot) *v.* To hit with a quick, hard blow.

swirl (swûrl) *v.* To spin around; to turn around rapidly.

symbol (sim´ bəl) *n.* Something that represents something else.

T

tannery (ta´ nə rē) *n.* A place where animal skins are treated to become leather.

tepee (tē´ pē´) *n.* A tent shaped like a cone. A tepee is made from animal skins stretched over poles. Native Americans who lived on the plains used tepees.

tempest-tossed (tem´ pəst tost) *adj.* Thrown around by a storm; storm-tossed.

tend (tend) *v.* To take care of; to care for.

texture (teks´ chər) *n.* The look and feel of something.

titanic (tī tan´ ik) *adj.* Great in size or power.

toss (tos) *v.* To move back and forth.

transfer (trans fûr´) *v.* To move something from one place to another.

treasure (trezh´ ûr) *n.* An item of great value.

tremble (trem´ bəl) *v.* To shake; to shiver.

tremendous (tri men´ dəs) *adj.* Enormous; huge.

trickle (trik´ əl) *v.* To flow in a small stream.

tundra (tun drə) *n.* A huge plain with no trees that lies in arctic regions.

U

unveil (un´ vāl´) *v.* To uncover.

V

vendor (ven´ dər) *n.* Someone who sells things; seller.

violence (vī′ ə ləns) *n.* Strong physical force used to harm.

volcano (vol kā′ nō) *n.* A hole in the earth that throws out smoke, melted rock, and ashes, forming a mountain.

voyage (voi′ ij) *n.* A journey by water or through space.

volcano

W

wampum (wom′ pəm) *n.* Small, polished beads made from shells and strung together or woven into belts, collars, and necklaces. Wampum was used by some Native Americans as money.

warrior (wor′ ē ûr) *n.* A person who fights or is experienced in fighting battles.

water bug (wô′ tər bug′) *n.* A very large, slow-moving insect.

weary (wēr′ ē) *adj.* Very tired.

weight (wāt) *n.* How heavy something is.

wickiup (wi kē əp) *n.* A hut covered with grass or brushwood.

wigwam (wig wom) *n.* A hut made of poles covered with bark, leaves, or hides. Some Native American tribes built wigwams to live in.

wimp (wimp) *n. slang.* A person who is weak and afraid.

windmill (wind′ mil) *n.* A tall structure with sails on poles, or "arms," that stick out from the top and spin around using the power of the wind. When the arms spin, a machine inside grinds up grain or pumps water.

woodland (wood′ lənd) *n.* An area of land that is covered by trees; a forest.

windmill

> **Pronunciation Key: at**; l**ā**te; c**â**re; f**ä**ther; s**e**t; m**ē**; **it**; k**ī**te; **ox**; r**ō**se; **ô** in b**ou**ght; c**oi**n; b**ŏŏ**k; t**ōō**; f**or**m; **ou**t; **up**; **ū**se; t**û**rn; **ə** sound in **a**bout, chick**e**n, penc**i**l, cann**o**n, circ**u**s; **ch**air; **hw** in **wh**ich; ri**ng**; **sh**op; **th**in; **t͟h**ere; **zh** in trea**s**ure.

wordless (wûrd′ lis) *adj.* Silent.

worthy (wûr′ th**ē**) *adj.* Having enough value; deserving.

wring (ring) *v.* Holds or rubs together.

Y

yearn (yûrn) *v.* To wish for.

Yiddish (yi′ dəsh) *n.* A Jewish language.

yon (yon) *adv.* Yonder; over there.

Photo Credits

6, ©Layne Kennedy/Corbis; **28,** file photo; **38,** Penguin Putnam Books for Young Readers; **42, 43,** Tom Bean/Corbis; **44,** ©Jonathan Blair/Corbis; **45,** ©David Muench/Corbis; **46-47,** James L. Amos/Corbis; **48,** ©Jim Sugar Photography/Corbis; **49,** Richard T. Nowitz/Corbis; **50-51,** Gail Mooney/Corbis; **52,** David Muench/Corbis; **53,** Annie Griffiths Belt/Corbis; **54, 55,** ©Layne Kennedy/Corbis; **58,** Michael S. Yamashita/Corbis; **59,** Paul A. Souders/Corbis; **60 (t),** ©Jonathan Blair/Corbis, **(b),** ©Dave Chare Photography; **78,** Robert Frank; **80 (t),** The Art Institute of Chicago, Gift of Georgia O'Keeffe. Photograph ©1998, The Art Institute of Chicago, All Rights Reserved, **(b)** The Nelson-Atkins Museum of Art, Kansas City, Missouri. F75-21/45. Bequest of the Artist; **81 (t),** ©Jonathan Blair/Corbis, **(b)** Collection of The Whitney Museum of American Art. Purchase, with funds from the Print Committee. 83.13; **90,** Barbara Bruno; **144,** Sheila Hamanaka; **156,** file photo; **174 (t),** file photo, **(b)** ©Sigrid Estrada; **176,** The Metropolitan Museum of Art. Gift of Mr. And Mrs. Klaus G. Perls, 1990 (90.332). Photograph: ©1991 The Metropolitan Museum of Art; **177 (t),** The National Museum of Women in the Arts, Washington, DC. Gift of the Artist, **(b)** The George W. Elkins Collection, Philadelphia Museum of Art; **194 (t),** David A. Adler, **(b)** Robert Casilla; **210,** ©Peter Ziebel; **282,** Evelyne Johnson Associates; **312,** Betsy and Giulio Maestro; **315,** Jean Miele/The Stock Market; **332,** Mary Watson; **334,** The Butler Institute of American Art, Youngstown, Ohio; **335 (t),** The National Museum of Women in the Arts, Washington DC. Gift of Wallace and Wilhelmina Holladay, **(b)** Collection of The Birmingham Museum of Art, Birmingham, Alabama; Museum purchase in memory of Richard Kenneth McRae, with funds from family and friends; **374 (t),** Natasha Wing, **(b)** Robert Casilla.

Art Acknowledgments

Unit 4 (Fossils) Ed Miller
Unit 5 (Courage) Sylvie Wickstrom
Unit 6 (Our Country and Its People) Elizabeth Wolf